A Stroke of Luck

A Stroke of Luck

A Near-Death Story of Releasing Heartbreak,

Pain, and Trauma to Find the Life

Meant for You

Brenda Caster

For my dad, who was there for me always. I love you.

What Others Say
About Brenda Caster

Brenda Caster is a creative woman who suffered a massive *Wallenberg Syndrome* stroke that not many survive. This event compelled her to the other side and changed her life forever. Her return and journey in recovery have led her to speak words of hope in helping others find their way through life.

Brenda is a witty, wise, and wonderful woman with a compelling story. We each have our own stories of tragedy and triumph, but we often allow the tragedies to weigh us down, and we get stuck there. Brenda's triumph story will inspire you to see the incredible resilience of the physical body and the brilliance of the human Spirit. She is a role model for everyone who knows there is more to life than what has happened to us and that "everything always works out."

~ Lisa Warner, Author, *The Simplicity of Self-Healing*
ConnectingYoutoYou.com

Brenda is among the most unique women I have had the pleasure of knowing. She is intelligent, multi-talented, and beautiful from the inside out. Brenda has a certain magic. She transforms the ordinary into spectacular, and anyone, stranger or friend, who steps into her field will immediately feel her warmth and love for all beings. Brenda has courageously and intentionally turned a major health scare into an opportunity to truly live as the Soul she is. And Brenda does this with grace, trust, and love.

~ Shannon Valle, Holistic Chef
shannonsnaturalkitchen.com

When you first meet Brenda Caster, it doesn't take long to feel like you've always known her. She is a true light with a fun, firecracker personality. Brenda leads with her heart and is thoughtful, loving, and generous. I have not met many people who can maintain such resilience and positivity. When you know Brenda, you will hear her say, "Everything always works out!" she truly lives by this—so it does! Not to mention her creativity and vivid imagination. She is a talented spiritual woman creating beauty through her writing, music, quilts, and much more. Brenda is a fantastic human being. Her purpose on Earth and the message in this book will change the lives of many, and her impact will live on forever.

Julie Tunador, CHt
Transformational Hypnotherapist and Consciousness Coach
wideawakehypno.com

Contents

Acknowledgments

This book is a compilation of glimpses into my overall life. Every person and situation allowed me to grow, and they are appreciated. My dear friends and my intention group have all been instrumental in urging me to share my story. Thank you all! I love you—each and every one. I'd list the incredible number of names, but I'm afraid I might inadvertently miss someone. You've each got a place in my heart. My story is told, but it continues to develop with every breath I take.

Introduction

This is a book about life experiences that have given me the greatest opportunities to learn and grow. In writing it, I intend to provide you with a sense that things work out no matter what may befall you in life.

This project has been a long time coming—various obstacles popped up, seemingly from nowhere—but knowing things always work out, the timing of its release is absolutely perfect. Writing this and reliving these moments in my life have been cathartic in several ways. It has been emotional yet cleansing on several levels, and I believe it has given me a good overview of my life thus far. I can see where my life has been and the trajectory it's now headed because of these experiences. Seeing my life laid out like a puzzle and all the serendipities that have been and are at play is thrilling.

I might suggest that you keep in mind that everyone is, while fundamentally the same, different. Because there are over seven billion people in the world, there are approximately the same number of opinions. While my life experiences may differ from yours, we are essentially the same. As such, I believe you can not only survive but absolutely thrive under any circumstance.

My greatest aspiration for my words is that they will provide you with hope and the realization that no matter what comes your way, you are in control over your own life, and love is actually the answer to everything. I hope you enjoy it.

Chapter One

Growing Up

I was born as the oldest daughter to my parents, Bert and Beverley, in Montebello, California. My two sisters, Debbie and Denise, followed shortly after my arrival. We were an average family. Standing at around five foot nine, my dad had blue eyes and dark hair. However, by his thirties, he was going gray and balding. He reminded me of The Fonz, often carrying a pack of cigarettes in the chest pocket of his white T-shirt or rolled in his sleeve. His preferred attire included jeans with the hem rolled up at the ankle.

My mom, approximately five foot seven, possessed pretty brown eyes and wavy, reddish hair. My sisters and I shared similar features—fair complexions, freckles, and blue eyes. While I had naturally curly hair, they both had straight hair.

During our upbringing, we enjoyed marathon Barbie playdates. Chalkboard roads adorned the driveway, creating a course for our tricycles to navigate the various shops we had conceived. Our favorite establishment was the cracklin's—or pork rinds—shop. Grandpa was always eager to participate, patiently opening and reopening the door when we knocked at his shop. He would hand out homemade cracklins; in return, we would pay him with our imaginary money.

Mrs. Hawkey, an elderly woman in the neighborhood, would sit and talk to us on her front porch swing. She'd save rubber bands for our hair and make us special popcorn balls for Halloween. The Swopes lived across the street and always had those orange circus peanuts when we'd visit. Mrs. Swope would sometimes let me iron her pillowcases and handkerchiefs. I felt so grown up. Sometimes, I'd even get to dust. In retrospect, it was kind of a Leave It to Beaver neighborhood.

When I was young and not having a particularly good day, I told my mom and dad I wanted to go home. I knew somehow that this physical Earth was not my true home. They'd look at each other, and then there'd be the incredulous snort of laughter from my mom as she said, "Honey, you are home."

In a way, I knew that was true, but I also had a strong feeling my real home was someplace else. Throughout my life, when things get tough, I pray that I can go home. When things got really tough, I would beg.

I experienced an extraordinary amount of anxiety and stress beginning around age three. Things seemed to happen out of the blue. Sometimes, I'd sit in front of the TV watching cartoons, captivated by the unfolding story. From what seemed like out of nowhere, I'd be yanked up by the arm, unceremoniously spanked, and yelled at for reasons unknown to me. After that abrupt experience, I was made to sit alone on the front step to think about what I had done.

Boy, did I think? I would wrack my brain to figure out what I had done wrong. Why was I so bad? I mean, I must be bad to be spanked, right?

Events like this shook me, and I had no idea where they came from or why. It wasn't because I had a horrible childhood.

I was loved, and I knew it. I had lots of family and friends. These moments, however, gave me regular feelings of anxiety and stress. These off-the-wall moments may be why this event conflicted with my everyday life experience. I never felt entirely at ease on this Earth. Years later, I would find out why.

At the age of four, I was touched inappropriately by a small group of boys not much older than me. I had happily skipped down the block to play with them. The much-anticipated play date was suddenly squashed when they said I would have to take down my panties and let them look, or they wouldn't play with me. I was outraged. I stamped my foot as I adamantly refused.

The leader shrugged his shoulders. They turned their backs on me and started walking away. Are you kidding? I thought. I couldn't believe it. "Okay!" I shouted. This can't take forever, I reasoned, and I was escorted to the side of the house where I lay without my pants. What they did was uncomfortable, to say the least. I wasn't chuffed when a mom came around the corner, muttered, "Oh dear," and told everyone it was time to go.

I put my pants back on and went home. That certainly wasn't worth the promised play. My mom asked me what had happened when I walked through the door. I searched my brain, but earlier unpleasantness had already left my mind. "Nothing," I said. I had no idea what she was asking.

She then asked if I had taken off my pants. The light turned on in my brain. Oh, yes. I explained that I had to, or they wouldn't play with me. She took me in her arms and hugged me tightly as she groaned, "Oh no." She asked, "Why would you do that? Tears welled in my eyes.

I told her why: They wouldn't play with me—didn't she see?

As if things weren't bad enough, she said, "I am going to have to tell your father." I was horrified. The tears ran hot, and I buried my face in her embrace.

Whatever this was *must* be wrong if my dad was to be told. What did I do? I begged her not to tell my dad about this horrible thing I had done—whatever it was. He never did say anything to me, so I figured my mom took mercy on me. I was spared. The next day, however, I was taken to the doctor. He removed my pants and got busy looking *down there*. I was mortified. The shame I felt when speaking to my mom the previous day was nothing compared to this. This cemented it and brought shame to an entirely new level. I supposed this was my punishment for wanting to play with those stupid boys.

At age five, I went to kindergarten at Freemont Elementary. Mrs. Silverman was my teacher. I had made something in class that I was particularly proud of and couldn't wait to show my mom. I knew she would love it. When I got home, I ran upstairs, where I found my mom in my room doing something in the closet. I was breathless, hardly able to contain my excitement.

"Mom, look what I made!"

She said she was busy and kept on with what she was doing. She didn't seem happy, but I knew if she just looked at what I made, her day would turn around and be great. So, I persisted. "Mom, just look—just look at what I made!"

I was persistent until she finally snatched the paper from me and said, "Great, Brenda, but for every one thing you do right, you do fifty things wrong."

I felt she had slapped me in the face with her words. Tears of hurt, anger, frustration, and humiliation streamed down my face. I took the paper back and tore my masterpiece into shreds, thinking: *She just doesn't get it. No one does.*

The next day, Mrs. Silverman asked why I had ripped up my paper. I was flabbergasted and asked, "How did you know?" forgetting about the miracle of the telephone.

She replied, "A little birdie told me." I didn't much care for or trust birds after that—and they were everywhere.

I grew up Catholic and attended twelve years of parochial school. When I was in the first grade at St. Benedict's in Montebello, Sister Mary Concordia told my class that missing Mass was a mortal sin. For this, even our families would burn in the eternal flames of hell. That certainly left an impression.

20

We usually went to Mass on Saturday evenings. One weekend, our family went on a camping trip. On that particular Saturday, the sun grew heavy in the sky, and I started getting nervous. Wringing my hands, I asked my mom, "When are we going to Mass?"

"In a little while," she said.

There was an outside service where we were camping, and she said she would call me when it was time. But when the sun set, we still hadn't left.

Again, I asked my mom what was happening and was told we had missed the service but not to worry; we'd be going in the morning. Reassured, I played until it was time to get into the sleeping bags.

Morning came, campfire pancakes were consumed, and I was ready for Mass. "Mom, are we going to Mass now?" I asked.

"No, honey," she said. "We missed the service this morning, but we'll go when we get home tonight."

I relaxed a little. There was a plan. Once home, I was plopped into the tub, assuming I was getting cleaned up for church. I asked my mom, "What dress will I wear to church?"

"Oh, Honey, I'm sorry, but we got home too late," she said. "We missed Mass this week."

At that moment, I started screaming hysterically. Images of me and my entire family burning in the eternal flames of hell flashed across my mind. I was screaming at the top of my lungs in absolute terror. My mom had no idea what had happened. She quickly grabbed me up in a towel and rocked me, trying to calm me with her words. I wore myself out screaming and crying until I passed out.

I woke up in the morning with a complete sense of dread. Our fate had been sealed because I hadn't ensured we went to Mass. It was my fault, and my family would suffer this terrible fate. I would have to accept and somehow live with what I had done. To say it was a scarring experience is an understatement.

My dad loved to joke around and tease me, but I often didn't catch on to his teasing, believing whatever he said to be true. Throughout my parochial school days, he would say, *I'm going to send you to be a nun in the Congo*. Believing he had the power to do so, I was horrified. What had I done to deserve it? I had only imaginary visions of what the Congo might be like, but visions of Tarzan and Jane were at the forefront while I was wearing one of those long, hot habits the nuns wore in those days. I didn't realize until adulthood that he had been teasing me.

*

When I was about eight years old, we discovered that I had a hearing problem. My third-grade teacher was Miss Sagala. I remember her well. She was a kind person with a bit of a chunky frame.

Miss Sagala once wore the fashion of the time: a paper dress. It was a short-lived trend but all the rage in 1966. I thought it looked a little on the flimsy side. It turned out it was. Her dress ripped, and some girls went to the teachers' lounge to help her tape it up where it had torn on her ample frame. Things only worsened when she took the class outside for a fire drill.

It was a windy day, and as she walked backward, facing the class, her beehive hairpiece lifted and bobbed, bouncing back and forth on her forehead. She fought a losing battle to maintain her hair. The tape started coming undone from her dress. One hand desperately clutched her torn dress. The other tried to keep her hairpiece from blowing away. It was definitely a sight, and with my mouth hanging open, I stifled my giggles.

Miss Sagala was the one who discovered my hearing difficulties. I always did well in school, and one day, she asked me to move to the back of the room to break up a group of chatty boys in the back. I was happy to help her. if I weren't looking at a person, I couldn't hear them. At the back of the room, I had no idea Miss Sagala was speaking. It didn't take her long to realize something was amiss.

Shortly after that, I was on a bus with my mom. Not only had I never been on a bus before, but I also had no idea where we were going or why. We entered a large building in downtown Los Angeles. It was a doctor's office, and it was under construction. Lots of plastic drapes were hanging to keep dust and debris away from the patients. I was scared, but my mom told me to go with the lady and do what she said.

I was taken into what I can only describe as a vault-type room with a single light bulb over a table with games. It was a dark, scary place. The lady told me to sit in a chair, and the thick, heavy door was shut, leaving only that lone bulb for light. I tried not to panic.

She made me play what I thought were stupid games, such as putting shapes into same-shaped holes and various word games. Then, I put on earphones and listened to different sounds. I was happy to leave that place and be by my mom's side again when it was over.

Afterward, we walked into the doctor's office, and he looked in my ears. I was picked up and held sideways by the nurse and my mom with my head over the sink. A water gun was placed into my ear and fired. The water was immediate, shocking, and painful, and I started to cry.

Apparently, I had overactive glands in my ear canals, causing a continual wax buildup in my ears that inhibited my hearing. After they rinsed both ears, I felt like I emerged into a new world. Everything was *so loud*. I had to put my hands over my ears to muffle the noise. I had never heard all the white noise before clocks, buzzers, elevator dings, and people talking. It sounded like shouting to me.

I cried and asked my mom, "Why is everything so loud?" My head hurt, and my hands were over my little ears for weeks until I adjusted.

My sister, Debbie, and I received guitars for Christmas in middle school. I was thrilled. Our Lady of Perpetual Help—the school I attended—had a guitar group that played for one of the masses at the parish. I felt so happy to be a part of this elite group and practiced obsessively so I would do well. When it was practice time, I'd jump up from my seat, grab my guitar, and head out to the practice room, where I'd play my heart out with the other girls.

A few weeks in, the teacher stopped me before I entered the practice room. She said she was very sorry, but the girls took a vote and—though they all liked me—they did not like my guitar playing. Just like that, I was cut from the group. It hurt.

I was disappointed, but it did not deter me; I knew I could do it. My mom gave me a book with chords, and I would practice for hours each day, determined to show them I could do it.

That summer, my family decided to go to Washington State to see my great-uncle Lloyd and his family. I was not going to let this interfere with my guitar practice. Passionately, if not dramatically, I told my mom that I would not be able to go unless my guitar went with me. She reluctantly agreed, and room was made for my beloved guitar.

Once we arrived, I sat by the pool and strummed my heart out while singing softly for hours. My great-uncle heard me play. He listened for a while, and when I had finished strumming a song, I looked up and smiled at him, expecting some praise.

I will never forget when he looked back at me and said, "Why don't you sing and cover-up that shit?"

I was dumbfounded and more than a little pissed off. Like any self-respecting kid, I thought: *I'll show him! If he thinks my guitar playing is terrible, wait until he hears me sing.*

So, as he turned to walk away, I started playing and singing my heart out. He turned back and winked. I discovered I was a pretty good singer. Thank you, Uncle Lloyd!

At age fifteen, I started to put on a bit of weight. I didn't know how to deal with it. My mom told me about a weight-loss camp for girls and asked if I would be interested. I didn't know what else to do to lose the weight, so I eagerly agreed.

At the camp, I had three roommates. We attended mandatory classes on nutrition, exercise, and other physical activities. Unfortunately, I never ate anything my dad wouldn't eat—so broccoli and cauliflower were out of the question. I was often hungry since they mainly served vegetables. As the weeks went on, I became homesick too. Homesick, hungry, and sore from all the exercise was not such a good combo.

The mess hall was filled with all the girls from camp. Across from my group sat a bully and her clique. That particular day, I was exhausted, hungry, homesick, and sore. Perhaps sensing this, the bully started in on me. My patience was at an end. She was the type of girl who *loved* talking smack. She, for whatever reason, felt the need to pick on me.

"Does your mommy make your dinner? Does your mommy fold your clothes? Does your mommy wipe your ass?" She went on and on with stupid, childish taunts that I let get to me.

I snapped. I stood up, slapped my hand on the table, and said through gritted teeth, "My Mother Does NOT!" I turned my back and walked out. There was a pay phone near my room, and I stopped and made a *collect call* to my mom, demanding I be taken home immediately. Crying, I threatened to walk all the way home if no one came for me.

I went to my room, locked the door, lay on my bed, and cried. I cried and cried, and then I cried some more. My counselor, key in hand, came in and tried talking to me, but I was sobbing with no end in sight. Finally, she left me to my tears.

A little while later, I heard the door open. It was my dad. I was never so happy to see anyone in my entire life. I threw myself into his arms, ready to go home. He took me in his arms for a few minutes, and then, holding me at arm's length, he looked into my eyes and asked what had happened. Had I been hurt? Raped? What was it?

I told him no. I just hated it there and wanted to go home. I was tired of being picked on. He said something that would stick with me for the rest of my life.

My dad said, "I will take you back home in a heartbeat, but you need to make a decision, and this decision could affect every single decision you ever make in your life in the future. It's easy to give up when things get tough," he continued. "But you can't give up whenever something doesn't go your way. If you want to give up, if you want to quit, I'm not going to love you any less. But you should ask yourself if you can stick this out. Whatever you decide is fine with me."

There were a few weeks left at camp. I decided to stay. This decision set the precedent for the rest of my life, and my dad had a big part to play in this. I realized I wasn't a quitter; adversity would not stop me.

*

After high school, I worked at McDonald's for a while. If you can believe it, they offered live entertainment there on Friday nights. This was way before drive-throughs entered the picture. My career as a breakfast cook was cut short. So began my days as a singer at McDonald's. On Friday nights, they put up a small stage in the corner with a stool and microphone, and I played and sang while people devoured Big Macs and fries. I was paid my regular cooking wage, which was high by all standards, at $2.76 per hour. This was my first paid singing gig.

Afterward, a small entourage of young girls would ask for my autograph. It felt amazing. I was asked to play for the intermissions of various beauty pageants around the area. I sang at weddings and anywhere I got the chance. I loved it.

However, even though I was busy with all the activities in my life, I felt this nagging void inside me. Though I was young, I wanted a husband. I wanted to be a wife and a mom, so I prayed.

Chapter Two

Steve

I never really had much of a dating life during or immediately after high school, what with working and life, but I always had friends. I went to church and Bible studies and prayed for a husband. My cousin Dawn called me one day and said her husband at the time, Scott, worked with the cutest single guy named Steve. She said I should meet him and that he had a *rubber face*. I wasn't exactly sure what to make of that.

Blind dates weren't exactly my thing, but the plan was for us all to go to church together and then back to their home for lunch. Steve was short but friendly, and he did have a rubber face. He could pull the skin several inches away from his face with no pain—it seemed to stretch just like rubber. Why he ever decided this was a talent that needed to be shared, I don't know.

Dawn and Scott left the room to make lunch, leaving us to talk and laugh. We were quick to get along with each other. All of a sudden, I felt this knowing inside that told me Steve was gay. I immediately felt comfortable with him because I spoke my mind and asked him.

He acted insulted and said, "Why would you ask me that?"

"I don't know," I said, "you just struck me as being gay. It doesn't matter to me."

He said that he wasn't, and we continued with the conversation through that afternoon.

After that, we started talking on the phone regularly. He said that he had been praying for a wife. He was a nice, funny guy, not exactly the dreamboat I was hoping for, but we seemed to want the same thing.

We all decided to go to dinner and then to a movie: a double date. We saw *Star Wars*, which had just been released. I felt comfortable with Steve. We were both very friendly, and he had an amazing sense of humor. That was May 25, 1983.

A week later, June 1st was my twenty-fifth birthday. Steve had planned a surprise party for me with Dawn as his willing accomplice. Before the surprise, he presented me with a double pearl ring at dinner. It was a wonderful birthday.

We were on the phone a week later and had a bizarre conversation. We talked about life and the future when he said something like: *and when we're married...*

I didn't really catch the rest of what he said because I was so surprised by what had come out of his lips.

I interrupted him and said, "Wait. Did you just ask me to marry you?"

He said, "Well, what if I did?"

"Did you?" I asked, a bit confused.

"What would you say if I did?"

"I'd probably say yes. Did you?"

"Well then, yes, I did."

"Well, okay. So, I guess we're getting married then."

"Yes, we are," he said.

"Okay, goodnight."

"Goodnight."

I put the phone back on the cradle and sat there, trying to digest what had happened. I loved him as my friend. None of this was exactly how I dreamed it would be. He was short, had sandy blonde hair—not exactly my type—and sadly, I was not in love with him. But I had been praying for a husband, and there he was. I thought to myself: *I'm twenty-five, and I want a baby, and here he wants the same thing, asking me to marry him. I'm sure it will be fine.*

I looked back over the last month of my life. I had met Steve on May 25. We went on a double date with Dawn and Scott seven days later. Then, seven days later, the surprise party; then, seven days after that, the proposal. *Isn't 7-7-7 the sign of God?* I asked myself.

I called my mom and broke the news to her. She was thrilled.

Steve was a nuclear engineer in the Navy and scheduled to be out to sea in early September. He wanted to get married before he left. He said he felt it would never happen if we didn't get married before he left.

We initially chose August 20 as the date, but my mom suggested August 27, which would have been her parents' fiftieth wedding anniversary. *Wow*, I thought, *what a special day this will be!*

So, the date was set, and we only had a few months to get it all together. It was already mid-June. There was only one small bridal shop in town. I purchased one bridal magazine, and my dream dress was on the cover. What were the odds this little bridal shop would have it? But they did! Now, I only had to find bridesmaid dresses.

Prom season was over, so most long dresses were no longer in stores. I called my favorite department store, Robinson's, and asked if they had long dresses. The woman sighed and said, "I'm sorry, I only have five, and they're going back tomorrow.

I asked what they looked like, and she said, "Four are exactly the same, and the fifth is similar. They are all mauve." That was the exact number of bridesmaids I had and the exact color for my wedding—mauve and silver gray. I told her to hold them and that I'd be by after work. Five different sizes, all perfect for my bridesmaids and maid of honor, except for the hemming. It felt unreal. Everything was falling into place. Things were moving so fast.

My mom—ever the resourceful woman—was on the phone trying to locate a venue. Most laughed. "The wedding is too soon," they said. "People usually reserve the venue a year or more in advance, not two months."

My sister had been married at the Little Chapel of the Roses in Bonita, California, and her reception was at the Admiral Baker Club in San Diego. My mom tried those places first but had no luck. She requested they please let her know if they had a cancellation. It didn't look good. Within days, both called and—by some miracle—had cancellations for August 27, but it would have to be late afternoon for the chapel and evening for the club—the *exact* time I wanted.

I still felt a lot of trepidation about the marriage, but everything was falling so effortlessly. *It has to be God*, I thought.

One day, I was at work. Dawn had the desk across from me, and I told her, "I hate having to go to the florist. It would be great if someone came to the office so I didn't have to do that."

As if on cue, the phone rang. I answered it, and a woman said, "You don't know me, but Mark, who does your nails, does mine too. I do flowers. I heard you might be looking for some for your wedding. I don't have a shop, but I could visit your office if you'd like."

We set a time. I hung up the phone and sat there with my mouth hanging open. No doubt, God's hand was at play.

The invitations were addressed and stamped, but I wouldn't put them in the outgoing mail at the office. The postman would come each day, and I shook my head no. I couldn't shake the feeling that this was a big mistake, but how could it be? Everything I wanted had fallen into place. It was, after all, what I had prayed for.

33

And don't forget that you're twenty-five now, and your child-bearing years are slipping away, I told myself.

Time was short, and if I was going to do this, I had to send the invitations out now. So, I did. But why didn't I feel elated?

My grandmother died in July, and my poor mother was left dealing with arrangements for her dear mother's death *and* my wedding at the same time. I busied myself making my magnificent wedding cake. Before I knew it, the big day arrived.

We were at the back of the chapel: flower girl, ring bearer, all four bridesmaids, my maid of honor, my Dad, and I. It was my turn after the entourage took their trips down the aisle.

I looked up at my dad, with what I assumed was that deer-in-the-headlights look, and said, "Dad, I don't want to marry him."

He laughed and said, "Oh, you're just nervous," with a little tug, he propelled me down the aisle. Outwardly, I had a smile plastered on my face, but inside, I felt sick to my stomach. With every step I took down that aisle, I knew in my heart I was making the biggest mistake of my life. But there I was, Steve was, and everyone else was looking at us. Once I saw Steve, I started to feel better and thought maybe my dad was right.

It's going to be okay, I told myself. I must have been wrong again.

My wedding night, however, indicated that I probably wasn't wrong. *We'll learn about each other's bodies over time, and it would all be okay*, I reasoned. I had to face the fact that, even though this decision might have been a mistake, I was the one who made it.

34

Chapter Three

Marriage

We were married only thirteen days when Steve was out to sea for what would be months. When he left, I cried and cried. Even though I wasn't in love with him, I still missed my friend, my husband. I'm not sure if I cried in part because he was gone or because of what I'd gotten myself into.

After a few weeks, I managed to pull myself together. I decided to throw myself into writing the endless wedding thank-you cards. I worked extra jobs to make it a very special Christmas for Steve when he returned. I had committed to this marriage and wanted to do my best.

Before Steve left for sea, he had been in a car accident. Unfortunately, he hadn't filed an insurance claim. Instead, he had made arrangements with the man who hit him and told me the guy would contact me and send money for the repairs. I'd never know why he had done this, but dealing with matters this way proved time-consuming and irritating. It became obvious the man did not intend to hold up his end of the deal, so I called our insurance agent.

The paint job on his car was oxidized, which is not cheap; the insurance definitely wouldn't have covered it. I worked many side jobs to surprise Steve with a new paint job. The "little dent," as Steve called it, turned out to be much worse, and it took months to resolve the electrical issues. I got the car back the night before he came home.

While he was gone, I wrote Steve long letters. I sent him cards, goodie boxes, and sometimes pictures. I made sure he received something from me every chance I had. There was no internet back then, so I worked tirelessly.

Dawn had told me that when men return from sea, sometimes it takes them a few days to adjust to everyday life, so I was prepared—or so I thought. She was a hostess at Filipe's Pizza Grotto in Lemon Grove and suggested that Steve and I visit her there on our way home. Dawn and I both laughed. We both knew I had other things in mind. I just wanted to be with my husband and make a Christmas baby.

Excited and nervous, I made the trek down to meet Steve's boat in my new, silky black dress, heels, and hat with a veil. I wanted to be his dream girl. I had fashioned a large red bow and placed it on the hood of his newly repaired and newly painted car. I knew he would be thrilled. I waited with the crowd of loved ones, anticipating our first embrace, our first kiss. Before I knew it, there he was, walking toward me.

His limp embrace and obligatory peck on the cheek left me speechless. Not knowing what to say, I lamely said, "Hi."

He said, "You're wearing a hat." I said, "Yes, I am."

"I hate hats," he said.

I said nothing.

"You're wearing heels."

I said nothing. What could I say? No matter what I did, his five-foot-four stature was less than my five-foot-five.

He said, "Let's go," I struggled to keep up with his pace.

I told him where the car was, and he stopped when he saw the bow. "What the hell?" His words dripped like poison.

"I had it fixed and painted for you for Christmas!" I said excitedly.

He looked at me and said, "*This* is my Christmas present?"

I was absolutely stunned by his reaction, but I let it pass. I remembered the adjustment time that Dawn had told me about, and I said, "No, it's just one of them."

He held his hand and said, "Give me the key." He grabbed the bow, opened the door, and tossed it on the floorboard. He slid into his seat, muttering about how embarrassing that was.

The long ride home was awkward. As we approached the Lemon Grove area, I said, almost as a joke, "Dawn's working tonight and said we should stop by for dinner."

I *never* anticipated his enthusiastic "YES!" I could not have been more stunned. As we walked into the restaurant, Dawn, equally surprised, greeted us and led us to a table. She looked at me as if to say: *What the hell are you guys doing here?* I excused myself for the ladies' room, and Dawn scurried behind me to say, "Bren, I was just kidding!"

"I know," I said, "I was, too, but Steve thought it was a great idea."

Dawn, looking concerned, said simply, "Oh." I tried not to cry.

The day had not gone as I had hoped, and the night was shaping up to be the same. We ate our dinner with casual chit-chat. The ride home was mostly silent, too, and when we got home, his obligatory lovemaking was even worse than on our wedding night. I felt deflated.

The next night, Christmas Eve 1983, Steve planned to go Christmas shopping and pick up a few things for my mom. Before he left, he said he wanted to *talk*.

He told me he was disgusted by my appearance. In his estimation, I had gained at least fifty pounds since his departure and looked nothing like the photos I had sent. I had lost a little weight because of how busy I had been. And those photos he mentioned were taken two weeks before he got home. I was flabbergasted. His words cut deeply, reducing me to tears.

Finally, he left to go Christmas shopping. I just wanted him to leave. I lay on our bed and sobbed, wondering why I had chosen this for my life. Eventually, I cried myself to sleep.

A few hours later, I awoke to a book near my face and Steve saying, "You should read this."

The title of the book was Fit or Fat: You Too Can Be Thin.

Are you kidding me? I thought. My mouth hung open in absolute astonishment.

These "special gifts," as Steve called them, were incorporated around our tiny home in strategic places, so there was no way I would miss them. Whether he realized it or not, Steve's little gesture toward reducing my physical size only reduced my sense of self-worth and the love I thought I had for him.

This would be my life over the next two years. I don't recall a single holiday or special occasion that didn't end in tears.

I would put his robe in the dryer every morning to wake him with a warm robe and a hot cup of coffee. I'd prepare the breakfast of his choice and fix his lunch for him, but no matter what I did, it was never enough.

He didn't like things to be messy, so I'd ensured all the dishes were washed, dried, and put away. I ensured the floors were washed and vacuumed before showering and dressing for work. After work, I would stop by the store to get fresh vegetables for dinner—he liked them to be fresh—and whatever I would need for his lunch the next day. Because of his early workday, he got home much earlier than me. He had time for a nap and felt refreshed when I got home. I'd walk in the door, bag of groceries in my hand, kick off my shoes, put down my purse, and go into the kitchen to prepare his dinner.

When the evening meal was underway, I would pick up the newspapers, shoes, and shirts Steve had strewn across the floor during the day. I'd pick up the wet towels left on the floor or the towels that somehow missed the hook and landed beside the toilet. After dinner, he would simply sit in front of the TV while I cleared the table, washed the dishes, and cleaned the kitchen. When finished, I would sit on the couch near him, thoroughly exhausted. Within about five minutes, he would say, "Ready for bed?" Off to bed, we went, and the next day, it would start all over.

*

Steve had a large family, including seven siblings and their families, so it was decided that for our first Christmas, we would pick names, and each of us would buy a gift for one person. His sister, Nancy, selected my name. Steve and I decided to open one gift on Christmas Eve, and we chose the gifts from his family for the occasion. When I opened mine, I broke down and cried.

Steve looked at me, annoyed, and said, "Now what?"

I turned around the wooden sign with the inscribed words:

Love looks with the heart, and not the eyes.

He said, "I don't do that, do I?"

As if dared by his sister's gift, nearly every holiday or special occasion after that, Steve found some way to reduce me to tears. He would constantly insult my size and deride my body.

It just didn't make sense. One minute, we'd laugh and have a great time; the next, he'd insult me. If I asked him why we didn't have sex, his response was always the same: "Look at you!"

I remember one time he literally pointed, laughed, and ridiculed my body when I was changing to get ready for bed. That was the last time I ever changed in front of him. If he was in the room, I'd change in the closet. He routinely perpetuated that terrible sense of shame I had developed for my body since the abuse when I was four years old. It became a habit for him. After a while, I got used to it. I was amply endowed; there was nothing that I could do about it. I often wondered why he married me in the first place if he had found me so unattractive. It didn't make sense.

I tried to communicate with him and overcome our differences many times, but he would stonewall me. He never actually talked about his life, nor did he tell me the reasoning behind his judgmental actions.

Later that year, Steve got a call. He was being deployed again. This time, I didn't feel as bad as I had the first time he left. It wasn't the standard six-month-on, six-months-off basis as was the case for some boats. Steve was a nuclear engineer on the crew of a fast-attack submarine, and his schedule was erratic. He could be called in at any time.

What's worse, when he'd get the call, he'd have only about two hours to return home, pack, and report to duty. He'd wait until the last minute to call me and say he was leaving and wouldn't have time to see me. Then, within an hour, he'd be gone. The problem was I never knew when he would return after deployment. Steve might be gone for a day, a few weeks, or several months.

Despite all the uncertainty, I tried to keep the connection between us. I tried my best to please Steve and make him feel loved and cared for. I had to believe we could get through this and have a family.

*

My faith in our marriage was constantly being tested. One particular day, something completely changed my outlook. I noticed that he had started marking the food containers. He never verbalized it and probably thought I didn't know, but he was checking exactly how much I had eaten while he wasn't home. Realizing this, I was mortified. It was disgusting and felt so demeaning to me.

I discovered it one night when I was having ice cream. I looked at the container and saw his little mark. I was so disgusted with him that I almost threw up.

Still, I didn't want Steve to find out, so I kept eating. I finished the entire container, ran to the store, disposed of the empty container, and replaced it with a new one. Of course, I had to eat down to the new mark I made so he wouldn't know what I'd done. I spent the entire night making myself vomit, but he'd never know. I didn't want to give Steve the satisfaction of knowing. From then on, I would eat practically nothing in front of him, and I became a classic bulimic secret eater, bingeing and purging daily outside his ever-watchful eyes.

We'd been married just under a year when he got his separation orders from the Navy for the last year of his service. We moved near the base in Vallejo, California. When we moved, I had to quit my job, so I received unemployment benefits.

At that time, Steve wanted me to pay off a couple of credit cards. I was earning roughly five hundred dollars per month from unemployment. Steve expected half of that to go toward one credit card and the other half to another, leaving me almost no spending money. I smoked cigarettes at the time, but luckily, they cost less than a dollar a pack.

Before moving, we had three checking accounts: his, mine, and a joint account. However, Steve convinced me that we only needed one joint account. I had my doubts about that and told him so. I didn't want there to be any problems. He assured me there wouldn't be. Steve even told me I didn't need to work because of where we lived.

Before he left for work one day, I asked him for a dollar because I wanted to walk down and get a pack of cigarettes. He went ballistic.

"A dollar? *A dollar?!*"

Why was I surprised? I looked at him and told him not to bother. I would ask the neighbor who also smoked. She didn't think twice and just gave me a dollar. I told her I'd pay her back when I got a job.

Walking to the corner store, I decided never to ask Steve for anything again. The cigarettes cost ninety cents, and the paper cost ten cents. So, I bought the cigarettes and used the remaining dime to buy myself a paper and scan the classifieds.

*

I guess Steve realized what an ass he had been because when I got home, he had left a dollar bill sitting on the corner of the coffee table. I ignored it. I sat down and searched for jobs in the paper to make my own money. I circled the jobs that interested me, dressed and hit the pavement to apply to the places I had circled.

That afternoon, my phone was ringing off the hook with job opportunities. I accepted a position at Independent Savings and Loan in the secondary marketing department. I was very clear with them and told them I knew nothing about secondary marketing, let alone how to run a calculator, but they felt I was suitable for the job. They wanted me to start the very next day. I was so happy! I told them that I would be there in the morning.

When Steve came home, dinner was in the oven, and I was cleaning the house. He sat on the couch and watched me dust. I dusted right around his apology dollar. After a while, probably because I did not refer to it, he lamely said, "I left you that dollar."

"I saw that," I said. I left it at that.

The next day, I woke up and got ready for my new job. I was heading toward the door in my dress, nylons, and heels—not my usual state of dress for the day—when Steve stopped me. "Where are you going so early?" he asked.

"To work," I answered. I didn't even look back. I was never going to ask him for another damn dime. When my first paycheck came in, I went downstairs to the teller line and opened a separate

44

checking account again. We would go back to what we were doing before, with me paying for food and putting a set dollar amount in for household spending. I made sure I paid back the neighbor who loaned me the dollar.

Our marriage was lifeless at this point. We were simply roommates. We didn't have sex. Steve continued to make snide comments about my weight. My self-esteem was at an all-time low. The constant verbal and emotional abuse was wearing me down.

*

Even though we were essentially roommates, Steve and I planned to move to his home state of Wisconsin when he was discharged from the service. However, a few months before we were to make this move, he walked in one day and told me he wanted a divorce.

Needless to say, I was shocked. I knew the relationship was terrible, but I wasn't ready to end it.

"Why?" I asked.

He shook his head and said, "I just want a divorce."

I tried to get more details out of him, but no amount of talking made a difference. It was like talking to a stone wall. He felt it best I move home immediately.

So, I quit my job, loaded up the car, and headed back to San Diego. I felt hurt, confused, slightly glad, and defeated all at the same time. I still wanted a baby. I still believed that, somehow, we could get through this.

A few weeks later, Steve called and wanted to come down to see me. He said he wanted to talk. Had he changed his mind? I wondered. He came to see me, but absolutely nothing was resolved. I realized he just didn't know how to express his feelings verbally.

A week or so after that, he wanted *me* to see him so we could talk. Well, I was either the biggest optimist or the biggest idiot on the face of the planet because I went. We were sitting on the bed, and, as usual, his words said nothing. I grew extremely frustrated because he wasn't saying anything. Then he started crying, and my heart melted. I'd rarely seen him emotional outside of anger and passive aggression.

"How can I make this better for you if you won't talk to me?" I asked.

He told me he couldn't talk.

"The only thing I can think of is that you're gay. Are you gay? If you are, it's okay. I'll still love you."

He held his arm across his teary eyes and shook his head. No.

"Maybe something happened to you when you were young? Were you experimenting?"

"Once, in high school."

He told me he did not have feelings like that; it was just a one-time experience. We ended up hugging and laughing. He assured me that once we moved, things would be different. So, we agreed to stay together.

46

Chapter Four

Wisconsin

Over the next few weeks, I kept busy, preparing for the trek across the country to my new life with a new family, including a little one—or four—as we had discussed before marriage. We purchased a used Chevy van, and Steve refurbished the interior, adding a bench seat that converted into a bed, bubble windows in the back, and a refrigerated cooler so we could camp anywhere. He did a great job. We decided to take our time traveling to our new life. The plan was to spend about a month en route.

Before we left, my mom had mentioned a place called Natchez, Mississippi, which she had seen in a travel magazine. I presented the idea to Steve. He responded with an emphatic no. He said we would stick to our planned route, seeing friends and family along the way, including my sister in Florida, before heading south to Disney World. Then, our final destination is Wisconsin.

There were no cell phones back then and no navigational apps like Waze. Reading maps is an art. When navigating, I hold the map to correspond bottom-to-top with my traveling direction. During our trip, I often held the map upside-down to make it easier for me to read. All was well until I said, "You need to take the next exit."

"Where are we?" Steve snapped, not believing the exit was so soon. I pointed to the map.

"You're so stupid," he said, sniping at me. "You're holding the map upside-down."

"I know," I said through gritted teeth. "You have to hold it that way to see where you're going."

He kept criticizing me until I said the dreaded word of finality: "Fine." I put the map away and zipped my mouth shut. We drove for hours in stony silence.

At some point, Steve asked again, "Where are we?"

Knowing I had put the map away, I reached down and gave it to him without saying a word. As it happened, we weren't far from Natchez, Mississippi.

When he realized where we were, he said, "You did that on purpose!"

I looked at him and said coolly, "I told you where to turn."

He ranted on and on. Having had just about enough of him, I snapped. "Then turn around!"

He changed his tone, and we kept rolling toward Natchez. It was a beautiful place. Surprisingly, Steve liked it so much that we stayed for a few days. Disney was out, but—having lived in Southern California most of my life, I visited the Magic Kingdom in Anaheim on numerous occasions—I was good with that.

In October 1985, we arrived at Kenosha, Wisconsin, where we rented a beautiful home with a pool. Steve had landed a job as a nuclear engineer at a nuclear power plant in Zion, Illinois, just a few miles from the Wisconsin border. Still, he had to regain the certification he lost when he left the Navy and was decommissioned. Steve also wanted to finish his engineering degree in Applied Science, so he enrolled in night school. The move to Wisconsin was so that he could attend a state school free of tuition as a resident born there.

Steve told me not to work, so I stayed home, trying to fill my time. By nine o'clock each morning, I was done with my household duties. Everything was scrubbed and vacuumed, the laundry was done, and I had nothing to do. Every day, I'd strike up conversations for hours with anyone I met at the grocery store. I got pretty lonely.

Steve would leave early for work, come home for a quick dinner, and then go to school afterward. He often stayed late to study and wouldn't get home until nearly midnight. I would try to stay up, but he'd always said the same thing: *You don't have to stay up waiting for me.*

Why wouldn't I? I hadn't seen my husband all day long. We still weren't having sex, and of course, there was still no baby. I asked him what his thoughts were on artificial insemination. He said it was gross.

I said, "No one would know. Your sperm, my egg, our baby." The "turkey baster," as he called it, was not for him.

I read about the timing of sex with ovulation for guaranteed results and came up with a plan. I said to Steve, "If you have sex with me for these seven days, I will never ask you again." He was excited by that prospect and seemed on board with the plan. However, on Day One, he had a headache. The plan failed before it started.

I thought we should sleep in separate rooms. No, he said; that's not how it was supposed to be, at least in his mind. What would people think?

"First of all," I said, "I don't give a rat's ass what people think. Secondly, I'll tell *you* how it's supposed to be: A man should want to make love to his wife."

He became subdued and said, "Yeah, you're right."

Maybe it was all the focus on having a baby, but Steve suddenly wanted me to look for a job and find us a home to buy. He told me things would be better once we got our own home.

I landed a job in North Chicago doing accounts payable. Shortly after, I found a beautiful Queen Anne Victorian home on a double city lot two blocks from the lake. It was built in 1890 and needed work, but I loved it. Steve agreed wholeheartedly, and I started believing things would be better once we had our own home. We secured the house under contract and organized the team to help us. I could almost see the kids running around the yard.

We were packing and getting ready to move into the new house when I got this overwhelming feeling that hit me like a brick. Steve was going to leave me. I looked at him and asked, "Are you going to leave me, Steve?"

He was taken aback. "What the hell is wrong with you? Why would you say that?" he asked.

"I don't know," I said. "I just feel like you're going to leave me, and if you're going to leave me, then you need to tell me right now."

"What's wrong with you? Have you got a screw loose?"

I finally let it go, but I couldn't shake the strong feeling that something was off, and here we were, getting closer to the closing date on our new home.

We went to the title company office when it was time to close on the new home. Our attorney reviewed the papers and handed the documents to us to sign. Steve asked me, "Are you *sure* you want this house?"

That terrible feeling came over me again—that Steve would leave me. I looked at the others and said, "Can you give us a minute?"

Our chairs had wheels, so we rolled a few feet from the table. A look of shock and disbelief passed across the faces of all parties in the room. I imagine they were all thinking of the worst-case scenario. It could all fall apart mere moments before the close.

"Steve," I said, regarding him. "I love that house, and the *only* reason I wouldn't want it would be if you have something you need to tell me. Are you going to leave me?"

Again, he said, "No, I'm not."

"All right, then let's buy the house."

That night, we celebrated by buying some Chinese food with the overpayment of interest we received in cash, and we ate it sitting on the floor of our new house. We hired a carpenter to install kitchen cabinets to match the butler pantry. The appliances were ordered, and the upstairs and stairway carpets were on the way. We discussed plans to restore the beautiful Queen Anne home. I felt lighthearted when we headed back to our rental that night. The movers would be arriving early in the morning. It would be a long weekend. I went to sleep that night with a smile.

*

We woke up early the next morning. Even though we had a ton to do, I felt so happy and foolish that I thought Steve would leave me. He signed the papers. We bought the house, and we were moving together into our future.

We woke early. When the movers showed up, we jumped into action. Once everything was moved in, I stayed behind at our new home to settle us for the night. The next day, we started early again, and we didn't finish until late evening. It was an exhausting but exciting weekend.

Monday morning, I woke up feeling terribly sick. Since we were fairly new to Wisconsin, I had no idea where to go that took Steve's healthcare insurance. So, I called him at work and asked. To my surprise, he said, "I'll be right there!"

Taken aback, I said, "I'm not dying. I can drive. I just need to know where to go." Oddly, he insisted he would come home and drive me to the doctor.

The doctor said it was probably just a bad cold, but he wrote me a prescription and sent us on our way. Steve drove me back home and tucked me in on the couch to rest. I looked at him with so much gratitude and said, "I'm lucky to have you."

He said, "No, you're not."

"Yes, I am. You're taking such good care of me. I love you. Thank you for taking such good care of me."

I fell asleep shortly after he left for the pharmacy, sometime mid-morning, feeling safe and warm and loved. I woke up around twilight, and he still wasn't home. I felt groggy and foggy in the brain, unable to get my bearings. I was starting to wonder where Steve could be when, as if on cue, the door opened. He walked in and stood at the entry of the parlor that was my makeshift sickbed. My face lit up with a smile.

"Hi," I said. "I was wondering where you were."

Steve walked into the room, handed me my prescriptions, and said, "You were right. I am gay. I want a divorce."

I just laughed. "Yeah, right, good one, honey."

It had to be a joke. We had just bought the house together. As I was opening my prescription, he said, "No, I'm serious."

"That's ridiculous," I said, confused. "We just bought this house three days ago. Why would we get this house?"

"I'll be right back," he said. He got up and disappeared outside. A minute later, he came back in—smoking a cigarette!

"Are you kidding me?" I said. "When did you start smoking?" He could spring for a pack of cigs since it was for himself. Not only was he a closet homosexual, but he was a closet smoker, too. *Who the hell is this guy?* I thought. I was beyond stunned.

Things only got worse as Steve revealed his plans. In his mind, I loved the house, so he wanted me to have it, even though he had planned to leave.

"How exactly am I going to pay for this?" I asked. The heating bills alone were too much for me to afford on my new $7.50-per-hour job.

"Well, you could afford it better than I," said the nuclear engineer. "You do crafts."

To say I was dumbfounded might be the understatement of the century. It was confirmed: I had married a moron.

His big plan was for me to live in and pay for this home based on my crafting ability and low-paying job alone. He said he would come over and mow the lawn while I did his laundry and cooked for him. He would come and go at will, while I, on the other hand, wouldn't know when he was coming or going or where he was even living. This way, I wouldn't interfere with his life.

No room for discussion was allowed. I opened my mouth to speak, and he threw his hands up and said, "I can't talk to you when you're like this!"

In typical fashion, he got up and walked out the door. I don't exactly know how long I sat there, but at some point, I realized my mouth was still hanging open from the shock.

I was beyond words. I could hardly believe this bizarre set of circumstances. While I sat there, my world seemed to tip sideways. I lost all track of time and, for that matter, reality. I would sob, cry, and wander through the endless sea of half-unpacked boxes for the next several weeks.

*

Steve showed up again a few weeks later, but apparently nothing had changed. Another absurd conversation ensued.

"What do you want?" I asked.

"Nothing," he replied. "I don't want anything."

I said, "So, you don't want that?" I pointed at a box of his stuff. He replied, "Well, that's mine."

"Okay, once again, what do you want?" I asked.

"Nothing."

I pointed to another item in the room, "So you don't want that?"

He again replied, "Well, that's mine."

I said, "Well, what exactly do you want?" Again, the same response.

Being a fairly astute woman, I realized this conversation was going nowhere. I realized long ago what Steve's philosophy was: what's his was his, what's mine was his, and what's ours was his.

According to Steve, I should "just get over it." I was not the only one ever to have married and divorced a gay guy, he said. To top it off, he was mortified that I would tell my family that he was gay. He begged me not to tell his family and said, "It's all I have left."

I told him I was not going to lie to my family. I agreed not to tell *his* family. He could say to them whatever he wanted, for all I cared. However, when I spoke to his sister and told her of the upcoming divorce, she asked if he was gay. It turned out his family had known all along. Still, when pressed, I said nothing to the rest of them except, "You'll have to ask Steve."

The absurdity of it all continued. A few days later, Steve said, "I'm taking a vacation. I'm going to Key West. I need a break from all of this!"

He needed a break? Seriously?

I realized later that the vacation was financed using our joint credit cards—the ones I wasn't allowed to use. It was a sizeable amount, so apparently, he and his friend had a good time. While he was gone, I kicked it into gear to leave the house. My dad had sent me money, and I hired movers to come pack my things and move me out. Steve could live in that house. I was done.

Steve's sister told me I could stay with her and her family for a little while—which I did. Eventually, I moved in with Steve's cousin, who had a dairy farm in the area.

Even though I was hurting deeply, working on the dairy farm left me little time to dwell on my woes. Farm life was a hard life. The work never stopped. The work began early in the morning and ended in the evening. I would prep for breakfast, clean the house, and take care of the laundry while Steve's cousin would bring the cows into the barn and start the milking.

After I changed out the first of many laundry loads for the day, I'd put on my mud boots and head to the barn. My job was to scrape the manure off the alley, the concrete path into the barn where the cows were brought in and out.

After completing that job, I'd feed the cows their special pellets. Next, the calves needed to be hand-fed with a giant bottle. Then, the chickens had to be fed; the barn cats received a large dish of fresh milk. When those chores were done, I'd clean the milk room and equipment before heading back to prepare a massive breakfast. After breakfast? You guessed it—more chores.

The day chicken carcasses were brought into the kitchen for me to pluck and cook, I quit my job of feeding them. But perhaps the worst thing on the farm was an incident with the cow. I wasn't hurt, only shaken. Being licked by a cow just about did me in, but I survived my brief stint of farm life.

A few weeks later, I drove back to Kenosha for the court date for our divorce. I hadn't seen Steve in a while before that. I was wearing heels, something he always hated because of his short stature. When I walked in, I was greeted by some guy I didn't recognize. I looked down at the man, thinking: *Who the hell are you?* It took me a minute before I realized it was Steve. I couldn't believe it. This could *not* be the man I had married!

Steve looked completely different, like a little old man. I realized I had always looked at him through the eyes of love and never noticed those things about him. Evidently, that had changed, and I saw him for what he indeed was: a liar and a thief, a skinny little man who never gave a damn about me.

In court, his lawyer told the judge that Steve would valiantly assume all the joint debt and graciously give me the car. However, since our savings were now in his name alone, it was easy for his lawyer to secure it for Steve. It was *his,* after all, the lawyer told the court. He went on to portray me as a squandering wife. Ultimately, I had no assets and a staggering amount of debt. I was awarded a one-time payment of two hundred dollars: gas money to leave the state. Steve had planned this well.

Chapter Five

After Steve

Thank God for family. My uncle came and helped me move. With the U-Haul packed to the brim and the Honda in tow, he drove me across the country while I sobbed the whole way. I was hurt, angry, and bitter.

I had called my mom to ask if I could move home when this happened. I had no place else to go. I don't think having her twenty-eight-year-old adult daughter move home was exactly in her plans, but she let me return.

I was navigating a terrible depression. I had no job no money, and the creditors were constantly calling me at my mom's to collect on the delinquent bills—all thanks to Steve. The stress of it all was killing me.

The stress got so bad that it began affecting my vision. I developed what I later came to know as *reverse tunnel vision*. It was terrifying. Everything directly in front of me I could not see. It's as though a clogged-up straw was in front of my eyes. I could see what was on the periphery but not in front. I freaked out and ran into the bathroom to look into my eyes, and to my horror, I could *not* see my face. No matter how I turned my head, I could see nothing directly in front of me. I stumbled back to bed, shut my eyes, and resigned myself to whatever was happening.

I thought: *Fuck it. I don't care anymore. God, fix this or don't. I'm done.*

When I woke up the next morning, my vision was normal again. Yet, I was still in a state of dark depression and fear every time the phone rang. My mom kept checking on me to see if I was okay, but I couldn't cope with another damn thing. I just wanted to go home or be gone from this world. My avoidance got so bad that I pushed a dresser in front of my bedroom door to keep my mom from coming in. I only came out in the middle of the night when I knew she was asleep, then barricaded myself back inside the dark hole that was my room.

Steve was supposed to maintain my car and health insurance until the divorce was final. I guess the lure of pinching yet another penny was too much for his greedy nature because he could not fulfill that portion of the court order.

Meanwhile, I was trying to get my own car insurance. I finally found an agent, but there were some difficulties. He told me it would be cheaper to split the policy with Steve. Unfortunately, they were going through a computer change and it couldn't be done until after it was resolved. The only option was for me to pay him under the table in the meantime. The agent assured me that he would fix the problem as soon as he could. But still, that computer problem dragged on.

It wasn't until I got into a car accident that I found out it was all a scam. It turned out I had no coverage. The agent had given me a bogus policy number. I dumped him and got a new agent. During that debacle, I tried to renew my driver's license, only to find it had been suspended for years. I wondered if the disasters would ever stop.

I didn't make it any easier on myself. Shortly after the DMV nightmare, I thought comforting myself with food might be a good idea. It seemed like the only thing I had control of anymore was what I put in my mouth. I didn't feel worth anything at that point in my life. I felt like I didn't deserve anything. I just stuffed my feelings deeper into my body with each meal.

I knew I needed to find some spiritual stability, so I started going back to a small home church in Carlsbad. I met a woman who needed a house sitter. She approached me after church, discussed it, and so began my career house-sitting.

It was nice being alone and not having to engage with anyone—not being responsible for much of anything. I thought the two-week house-sitting stint would end my new career path, but God had other plans for me. Just when one house-sitting job was about to end, another came up. I ended up house-sitting for almost a year.

Eventually, I moved in with my cousin and his family in San Marcos. I got a job at Green Horizon Landscape near their home and a post office box. I changed the address from my mother's house to my new post office box so she wouldn't be burdened with the increasing amount of pink mail. I don't know who decided pink would be a good color, but it certainly stands out and lets the world know: *collection notice enclosed.*

At that time, I had no phone number. I didn't have a landline, and there were no cell phones then. The creditors called everybody I had ever listed on credit applications for a reference to collect from me. I'm sure my friends and family regretted the day they ever agreed to be listed.

I was just trying to survive and get back on my feet, so I stuck my head in the sand and didn't respond to any of their letters. It got so bad that I retrieved mail from my post office box only in the middle of the night. I was sure a collection guy was waiting to serve me with papers.

The breaking point came one day when I was at my mom's. One of the creditors caught up with me at her house, demanding money immediately for a refrigerator I had purchased a year and a half before for Steve's cousin in Wisconsin. The creditor threatened me. I had no home or money.

I was morbidly obese, and I said to the creditor, "All I have is the blood running through my veins, and if you'd like to come get that, it's yours. If you want the refrigerator, then go get it!"

I gave the creditor woman the address to Steve's cousin's house in Wisconsin. I realized the worst thing they could do to me was kill me. I reasoned that might not be such a bad thing after all.

Shortly after that, I met with my dad. He sat me down and said, "Hon, you must deal with this. Sit down, determine what you owe and can pay, and write all the creditors a letter. Explain what has happened and what your plan for repayment is. That's all they want. You've got to deal with this. It's not going to go away. If they agree, great. If not, well, you might have to file for bankruptcy."

So, I did just that. I took his advice. I dragged out the giant black trash bag full of notices from creditors and sorted them. I figured out how much I owed each creditor and developed my plan to pay each a whopping eleven dollars monthly. I would add that eleven dollars to the amount being disbursed once a creditor had been paid off and split it among the rest until all were paid in full.

Most of the creditors responded with more threats. Only two of the creditors responded kindly, even offering words of encouragement. I was able to pay them off right away. As for the rest, bankruptcy was inevitable.

I planned to file a Chapter 13 bankruptcy—where you work out repayment. My dad said no matter what you file, a bankruptcy will show up as a bankruptcy on your credit. He advised filing a Chapter 7 and simply starting over. I felt like a complete loser. It was a humiliating experience. I thought I couldn't sink any lower than this.

I was grilled by the trustee who officiated the bankruptcy on the day of my hearing. It was horrible, but in the scope of things, it lasted mere minutes. As bad as the ordeal had been, it had finally concluded. Perhaps now I had a chance to start over.

Chapter Six

Starting Over

Working at Green Horizons Landscape didn't last long, and I moved on from that place without a backward glance. Not too long after the bankruptcy, I called my dad and asked him if he needed any help. He was happy to hire me again, and I was happy working with my family. The timing was perfect.

At Caster Management Company, we specialized in managing manufactured home communities. I was the general office manager and kept the books for our communities. It kept me busy.

In the early nineties, the elderly owners of one of the properties we managed decided to sell. My dad bought it and formed the corporation Oak Tree Ranch, Inc., eventually renaming the park Oak Tree Ranch.

Oak Tree Ranch spanned ninety-two acres in the foothills of Ramona, California. The park was built in 1965 and featured 49 lots—though it was permitted for 255 lots. It was a beautiful property filled with mature oaks and fresh, crisp air. Just being on the property, you felt like you were camping. It was a special place.

We moved our El Cajon office into the old farmhouse in Ramona and managed the property from there while still managing many California properties. In addition, my dad was also a manufactured home dealer, and I was a licensed manufactured home salesperson. Slowly but surely, as the older, metal-sided, single-wide homes came up for sale, we'd purchase them if we had the chance and put in a newer manufactured home.

The nineties weren't the best of times for lending, and sales were slow. Despite that, I worked seven days a week for years without time off. Doing sales in this slow market was tedious work. It was the most stressful time of my entire life. After seven years of it, I was fried.

My dad came to me and said he needed to cut back, so I had to choose whether to stay or go. If I stayed, I would continue the meager, time-consuming, and exhaustive sales efforts and be responsible for all the books, clerical duties, and property management. I didn't have any life as it was. It didn't take me long to make my decision. I made my exit.

At forty, I retired from the security of my nine-to-five life. Though I occupied myself with gardening and canning, it just wasn't enough to keep me busy. Eventually, I grew bored. A friend who managed an escrow office asked if I would help clear up a *few* old mobile home escrow files. *Sure*, I thought. *No stress there.*

Well, a "few" turned out to be a room filled with old files that still had money in the escrow. My job was to determine whether the title for the home had, indeed, been transferred. If so, we were to issue the refund and close the file—which would close the escrow—so the file could go to storage. If not, I would do what it took to make the transfer and disburse whatever money was in the escrow. It was like playing detective.

The stress of the escrow office was not for me. Fortunately, I was able to take a box full of files home and do what I needed to do. At night or on weekends, I would go to the escrow office, get on the computer, cut checks, and leave a neat pile on the escrow officer's chair. When I returned the following evening, I would get the signed checks ready to mail, close out the files, mark the box For Storage, and pack up another box to take home. It was great working when I felt like it.

My escrow detective work was winding down when my dad contacted me. This was in the late nineties. He and his wife, Deanne, wanted to take me to lunch. He told me they were ready to start the expansion of Oak Tree Ranch and asked if I wanted to come back and help him.

I firmly said no. I honestly didn't know if I could do it. Having worked for my dad in the past, I knew it would be a ton of work. I didn't think I had it in me anymore. They were disappointed.

They invited me to another lunch a week later, and I was approached again. Again, I said no. I did indeed feel bad for turning them down. This was my dad's dream. He had spent considerable time and money preparing for it, maneuvering many obstacles to get this project off the ground. It weighed heavily on my mind, and I couldn't help but think of the countless times my dad was there for me—the number of times he pulled my rear out of the fire—and his seemingly endless love for me, although I am quite positive, I caused him great frustration throughout my life.

How could I *not* do this for him? I struggled with this decision and spent about a month working to push beyond the burnout that caused me to retire in the first place. I found that place inside myself, summoning every ounce of inner strength. When I felt solid in my decision, knowing I could take it on, I called him and let him know I'd do it. He was very happy with the news. It was like he felt that things were finally on track, and it was a go. No looking back now.

The voluminous job at the escrow company was down to a small box of what I called "the weird ones," about a dozen. These were the ones that would most likely require the legal department to get involved. I had set up a system so new files coming out never ended up in the back forty again, so my adventures in escrow land were ending. I wrapped up the last bit of work there and made the transition.

My dad had moved his office to San Marcos, near where he lived, but a date was set when we would relocate the office back to the property in Ramona. The wheels were in motion. I was back to doing books and managing the park. Our efforts to bring this beautiful community to its full potential would require all our time, so our management of other properties was extremely limited.

Building this property out was no small feat. A valid permit apparently means nothing to a county needing funds. The process took not only lots more money but also *years* of negotiation. Finally, Phase 2 was completed. Now owning the *only* rental park in the county with newly manufactured home sites, we invited all the dealers in the county to place new homes in our community. Three of the biggest dealers each took three sites. Our architectural standards were pretty stringent, requiring all improvements— garage, landscape, concrete—to be made promptly. It was a far cry from the *plop and set* they were all used to.

Our homes were all *pit set*—meaning the site was excavated, so the home was below grade. My dad worked out an innovative system that is still in use today and gives the appearance of a stick-built home. When finished, these homes would be amazing. Nine homes would be in full swing.

Unfortunately, once the homes had been built, there was not a lot of marketing going on. Many excited people would inquire about the homes for sale and want to see them. The dealers had no presence on-site at all. No salespeople, no information flier was available, nothing. I answered all questions I could about the homes—even calling the dealer and letting the interested party speak to them. Most people seemed put off being instructed to go to the dealer's office some half-hour or so away and get pre-qualified so they could see the home.

I offered to show the homes at no cost to the dealer for their convenience—give out fliers or what have you. As I saw it, we had a mutual goal: Sell the home. They sell the home; I get a tenant. Win-win.

But they had no interest in my participation. This went on for what seemed like ages. I might have seen a tumbleweed roll by once. It looked like an abandoned project, with new homes empty and no construction going on. Interested people would come in and ask if the project had gone broke.

My dad and I were both very disappointed in the lack of dealer participation. He said, "I think we will have to fill this park ourselves."

I was less than thrilled. I did not want to return to selling houses, but what choice did we have? So, Oak Tree Homes Dealership was born. We put three homes in in June; by December, I had sold all three. We rolled those three into three more, and so on. The dealers cried foul. I told them everything: "If you would sell, I wouldn't have to."

Loans were plentiful back then, and while we always seemed to maintain three models, I now had people custom-ordering new homes. I was doing the books, handling the day-to-day management of the park, selling homes, ordering homes, and service writing for the houses, not to mention taking care of the escrow, title company, lender coordination, lease signings, etc.

Once again, I was working seven days a week. Eventually, we hired Glenda to answer the phones and pick up the slack. That helped some, but I was heading for burnout. I knew the signs from before, and I just needed to breathe. I told my dad I needed a few consecutive days off. I couldn't keep going at that pace. He agreed to give me Tuesdays and Wednesdays off.

It worked out. On Tuesday mornings, I would head down the hill and take care of things at the assessor and escrow before picking up my *lunch bunch* group of friends. We'd enjoy lunch and loads of laughs before I made my way back up the hill late Tuesday afternoon. Wednesday was housecleaning, grocery shopping, and laundry. Not much for rest and relaxation, but at least I had that time to do it outside of work.

When we finished Phase 3 of the park, we had more than sixty people waiting to buy. Unfortunately, the county threw a wrench in our plans when they decided to delay the final inspection—for almost a year.

We had ordered the homes but were not allowed to put them on the sites, let alone set them. They had been blocked and sat in the field, waiting for the county inspector to do their final check—which would take ten minutes. The delay was absurd. Finally, the State had to intervene to get this accomplished.

With the homes set and construction started, I was feeling more hopeful. And then, Freddie Mac tanked. Fannie May followed, and our FHA loans were all but gone. Conventional lenders dried up, and manufactured homes were such a small part of their portfolios that they felt it wasn't worth the stringent requirements and substantial financial commitments now in place.

Our waiting list of people all moved on. *It's taking too long*, they said. Phase 3 was a struggle to fill, but we pressed on with our plans for Phase 4. We always put our money back into the property, making improvements wherever possible. We were primed and planned to pull grading permits for Phase 4 in December 2007.

Phase 4, when even half-filled, would push us over the top financially, and we would be able to breathe.

In August 2006, my thirteen-year-old nephew, Seth, came for a visit from Florida. My gosh—how tall had he gotten! I hadn't seen him in years. Work had consumed my life.

His sister, my niece Allison, was in college. When did that happen? I missed so much of their lives. I vowed to make up for that and visit them at least once a year.

Shortly after Seth went back home to Florida, my sister, Debbie, called with news that would send us all reeling: Seth had cancer in his jaw. It was called *leiomyosarcoma*. I had a hard time wrapping my brain around what Debbie was telling me.

Ever the optimist, I *knew* he would pull through this. I offered words of hope and comfort, trying to stay upbeat. I put prayer chains in effect through emails, Facebook, and the Oak Tree Ranch Community. I started a weekly newsletter, delivered it to the residents in the park, and emailed it to friends who were praying for him to keep them apprised of his progress.

It never seemed to end. Things would go okay for a day or two, but then a test or scan would show cancer someplace else. He underwent massive doses of chemo, radiation, and surgery after surgery. Then, they found cancer in his liver. They told my sister and her family to take him home. There was nothing more to be done. My sweet nephew passed away in May 2007, surrounded by his mom, dad, sister, and grandma. I was devastated. How could this have happened? All our lives were changed forever that day.

71

Chapter Seven

Visions

Anytime I felt overwhelmed, I would slip out to the office porch, where the only thing that stood between me and peace of mind was a cigarette. It helped to clear my mind, which in turn helped me focus. If I were having a problem with something, these moments of quiet contemplation often would bring the solution to the forefront.

During this time on the porch, I began seeing a strange vision. I often looked across the street from the office, where a gorgeous grove of old oak trees intertwined with the homes from Phase 1. They swayed gracefully in the wind. However, the vision I kept seeing was all those oak trees burned in a surreal landscape of destruction. I kept asking myself: *Why am I seeing this? Is something wrong with me?* These disturbing visions persisted through the summer months.

On October 14, 2007, I was sitting at my desk, looking out the window. I saw a significant amount of smoke rising over the hill.

Where could that be coming from? I wondered. It wasn't long before Jerry, an employee and friend, came in and said, "You see that smoke?"

It all happened so fast. Before I knew it, Sandra and Glenda were at the office. They began delivering the notices I had prepared, alerting residents that there was a fire in our area and that it would be prudent to prepare for evacuation.

A friend and resident who worked at the Forest Service called with updates. The phones were ringing off the hook, and people were crowding the office, wanting to know what was happening. I did my best to evoke calm while urging preparedness.

My Forest Service friend called with the news I did *not* want to hear. The fire was coming at us, and they "had to let it go." They would not be keeping it at bay. We were now in mandatory evacuation mode. Our priority now was evacuating everyone. I prepared new notices alerting our residents there was a mandatory evacuation order in place, and they had to leave the property.

Sandra and Glenda delivered them door to door. Sandra canvassed Phase 1—the forty-nine original homesites. Glenda canvassed Phase 2—the fifty-three homesites of our first expansion—all before preparing their households for evacuation. I was so grateful for their help. I absolutely could not have done it alone. I phoned the seventeen resident sites of Phase 3, alerting them to the evacuation while continuing to field other calls and get further updates.

Once all the residents had been notified, it was time to call my dad, who was on vacation at the time. He was returning in his motor home when I called him. I asked if there was anything he wanted me to get for him. I got the files in his in-basket, his thumb drives, and the external hard drives on our computers.

Time was running out, and it was only me now. Outside, people were scrambling to load their cars and get out.

From my desk, I grabbed my Rolodex, list of bank accounts, tax ID numbers, and emergency contact info for our residents. I headed home, in Phase 3, to get my stuff together and get my beloved cats ready to roll. Once I was home, I realized no one had shut off the large propane tanks, so I headed out to do that. As if on cue, my dad called me back.

"Did anybody shut off the gas tanks?" he asked.

"I'm heading out now to do it," I said.

My drive around the park had an additional two-fold mission:

1. To see if I could find somebody who could help me

2. To make sure everyone got out, and if they needed help, I would help them

As I slowly drove around the park, I saw two people standing outside, staring at the flames over the hill coming at us. They had lost their previous home in the 2003 fire and were stunned at what transpired. I told them I was so sorry, but they had to leave.

One particular tenant I knew worked in construction. The place resembled a ghost town, so my options were running thin. I asked for his help with the tanks. He followed me without hesitation. While he went home to get his tools, I had an overwhelming feeling I had to get our permit files.

I ran back into the office, grabbed our drawer full of permit files, and threw them in the back of my car. When I got back to the propane tanks, two guys were there struggling to shut off the large valves. I was relieved when they accomplished that task. I was grateful for their help. Again—that was not something I could have done alone. I thanked them both and urged them to please leave the property before it was too late.

As the sun set, the wind was already fierce, and ash and smoke filled the air. It wouldn't be long before the flames were upon us. I returned to my house to get my stuff, get my cats in the car, and head out. I started looking around to decide what exactly to take. I realized absolutely nothing was important except my cats. So I grabbed a laundry basket of clean yard clothes that was sitting on the dryer and got the cats' carriers ready for loading in the garage.

I had just wrapped my big boy in a blanket and was holding him in my arms when the power went out, plunging us into darkness. Fortunately, I had some flameless candles around and had a hint of where I was in the house. I grabbed a flashlight and carried him to the garage. I dumped my poor boy headfirst into the carrier, snapped the latch, and loaded him in the car. Not a happy camper, my big guy was trying to slam his way out. Next was my little girl. She had always been rather skittish so it would have been a challenge even with light.

She was fine with me holding her, but when I started walking, she freaked out. Her claws dug into my chest as she tried to extricate herself from my grip. I said through gritted teeth as I pressed her closer to me, "I'm sorry, girl, but I'm not leaving you behind." She was in her carrier with the same procedure as her brother. I was a bloody mess, but my cats were safe and in the car.

My old PacBell phone was dead, and I had forgotten to charge it—no chance now, with the power out. To add insult to injury, my car's gas tank was riding on E. Could I make it to the gas station? I'm still here to tell the tale—so that's proof that miracles happen!

Getting out of the garage without electricity was another challenge. Unfortunately, I parked my SUV directly under the rope pull for the opener, so I had to climb on top of the car to lift the garage door open manually. The wind was so powerful that whenever I'd get it open, the garage door would crash down. Feeling the urgent need to get out of there, I looked around for something to hold it open. Not finding anything, I decided I would try one last time. I'd just ram through it with the car if it crashed down.

To my astonishment, it only came partway down, and I had enough room to squeak my car through. I could hear the door drag on the roof as I squeezed the SUV out of the garage and onto the road. My cats and I had escaped.

Looking through the rear-view mirror, I saw flames had crested the mountain behind me. It looked like lava oozing down the hill, devouring everything in its path, like the apocalypse. As I drove away, I had a horrible realization. I had been so busy helping others buy and arrange insurance for their homes that I had forgotten to buy insurance for my own.

I said out loud to my crying babies, "Well, kids, your mom eff'd up. Welcome to your new home."

I felt sick to my stomach and just prayed for the best. I ended up staying at my dad's house for weeks until the utilities were restored and we could reenter the property. I imagined we had lost everything. I couldn't even think about my house. What could I do about it anyway?

My dad managed to get back to the property and took an inventory of all that was lost. All forty-nine homes located in Phase 1—including all the infrastructure—and three of the fifty-three homes in Phase 2 were destroyed. It was the most significant density loss in the county. Our office and caretaker's home were lost as well. Our storage barns were both gone. The heavy equipment, work trucks, and half the RV storage area were gone.

I went through my emergency contact list and phoned people from morning to night to ensure everyone was okay. I also had the sad job of letting people know their home had been destroyed. My dad kicked into action and tirelessly worked to get new utilities trenched into the old farmhouse so we would have an office to return to.

The farmhouse we had been using as an office for years had fallen into disrepair and was used mostly for storage or temporary housing for laborers. Plans to restore the old gem had been on hold until Phase 4 was mostly filled. However, we needed it now. People came to help clean and clear the roads and do whatever they could so we could start work in earnest when we returned.

My house had miraculously survived. The day before the fire, I had hosted a friend's wedding there. So, two weeks before the fire, my friend and gardener, Jerry, had come over to work on the yard. He had removed old landscape bark and replaced it with pretty red mulch as part of the wedding preparations. If I hadn't had the landscape bark pulled out, my house would have gone up in flames, no doubt about it.

Pine trees at one end of my site were all burned up. The entire fence behind the house had melted, and a giant hole was burned in the fence in the front yard. The fire came within yards of my house, but somehow, the house was still standing.

Chapter Eight

The Aftermath

In the aftermath of the Witch Creek Fire that destroyed dozens of homes, it became apparent that this was only the beginning of the nightmare for all affected. Not only had fifty homes been lost, but also our income was literally halved overnight.

Checks I had ordered still hadn't come in, the insurance company wasn't responding, and we had only one phone— our new phones hadn't arrived yet. We had only an old card table turned desk and lines and lines of people needing to talk to me, including FEMA, Red Cross, Salvation Army, various church groups, residents, and county officials. My cousin Matt gave us desks, chairs, and accessories to use while we figured things out, including a new copier, computers, and office supplies. This lasted months; the drama, on the other hand, would last years. I went on autopilot, doing what needed to be done while trying to stay calm. We borrowed and borrowed simply to stay afloat.

Our insurance—what can I say? When I finally got through to someone, I said, "We've had a catastrophic loss! We need an adjuster out here now. The fire has devastated our property. I also need a copy of our policy."

The insurance agent said getting a copy of our policy was a lot of work, so I should just get a copy from my files.

I was dumbfounded. I said, "Ma'am, do you know what a *catastrophic loss* is? We've lost everything. The copy of the policy was lost in the fire. We lost half the park. Our office is gone. So, no, I can't get a copy from my files."

Seemingly unconcerned, she said, "Well, I'll see what I can do to get you a copy. It really is a lot of work."

Do you think that's a lot of work? I wanted to say. *Try losing everything in a fire.*

In the end, the insurance company stonewalled us, and we were advised our chance in a lawsuit against them would be fifty-fifty at best and would undoubtedly take *years*. San Diego Gas & Electric had been deemed liable for the fire, and we had no choice but to sue. The tree loss alone was assessed at around $10 million. The total value of damages was appraised at nearly $35 million. A myriad of class action suits were going on, but our community had suffered tens of millions of dollars in loss. We would stand alone in the suit.

We had to systematically lay off nearly everyone simply because we couldn't pay them. Eventually, only a skeleton crew—our longtime caretaker, Jessie, my dad, and I—remained. As one might surmise, I was stressed to the max. Long ago, I had given up any semblance of self-care. Between Mother Nature and time, the park lost its surreal atmosphere. Somehow, homes began to trickle in again once the arduous task of replacing the infrastructure in Phase 1 was completed. It would never be the same, but we pressed on regardless. We didn't have a choice.

Seeing the devastation as I drove to and from work in the golf cart was heart-wrenching, too. This was the horrible vision I had seen—like a war zone. I only wish I had understood it as a clue to beef up our insurance and back everything up—one of the oak trees burned for months. The fire department would come and dump water on it for an entire day, but a few weeks later, it would burst into flames again. It was unreal.

In January 2011, I looked in the mirror and wondered what the hell I was doing. To put it bluntly, I looked like shit. I felt like shit. I smoked like a chimney and ate continually. At fifty-two years old, I had bulked up to two hundred eighty-six pounds— roughly the size of a linebacker. This couldn't continue. Being a planner, I made a plan. I would quit smoking first thing, and by my birthday on June 1, I would have in place an eating and exercise program. This would be my year!

By March, I had quit smoking and was formulating the next part of my plan. Things were looking up. However, in May, a letter came from our attorney telling us that they could easily get us a $2-million-dollar settlement. I just about flipped. Were they insane? I couldn't even pay back what we had to borrow. My dad had left early that day, vacationing at his timeshare. I felt sick to my stomach. I dropped that letter on his desk and left it there. He could deal with it when he returned the following week. It was all too much: the responsibilities to our tenants, the shortcomings of the insurance company, not to mention quitting smoking. Everything seemed to push me closer to the edge.

81

When my father came home, it would be my turn for a week off. I couldn't wait! Sunday was Mother's Day. I went to work Monday. Little did I know that day, something major would happen, altering my life forever.

Chapter Nine

The Stroke

Have you ever taken a walk and just marveled at the sheer perfection of nature? It was that kind of day. Everything was in bloom and abundant beneath the brilliant Southern California sun. It wasn't too hot. It wasn't too cold. It was perfect. A gentle spring breeze blew. The birds sang their different versions of the same song. The fountain leading up to the office sounded melodic, too, with the trickling water from the bronze statues. At that moment, I felt happy to be alive.

I strolled up the walkway to the office on May 9, 2011, taking it all in, but as I neared the steps, reality derailed my euphoric moment. The phone was ringing. I raced to unlock the door and stepped inside. I snatched up the phone. It was a lender for a resale home wanting clarification and our assurances of their protection under that particular lease. I found the file and talked him through the various sections.

Suddenly, it was as if someone hit me upside the head with a baseball bat. Only, there was no pain. It was just this tremendous force on the left side of my head. I nearly collapsed.

At that moment, it felt like my brain actually split into two parts, and I clearly heard the dialogue from both sides. One side of my brain said, "What the hell was that?" The other side was carrying on the conversation with the lender as if nothing had happened. I knew my mouth was talking and answering questions for the lender and that my thoughts and explanations were somewhat cohesive, but at the same time, the other half of my brain was quite front and center, in control, assessing, and repeating, "What the hell was that?" I thought I should probably sit down before falling and maybe call 911.

I had enough wherewithal to sit down before I actually did fall down. I thought: *Okay, that was bizarre. But what was it?* Then, it happened again. *BAM!* Another homerun swing, only this time it was on the right side of my head. The force of this second blow was so intense that I actually felt my spirit leave my body. It knocked my psyche right out of me.

Up, up, up my spirit flew, at least three stories high. I looked down and could see myself sitting at my desk, talking with that lender. It all happened in slow motion, and I could actually see—or rather sense—my body falling forward onto the desk as it registered its life force was no longer with it. Then, I slammed back into my body with a jolt. I jerked upright, and once again, my brain felt like it was splitting in two. I could hear myself talking to the guy on one side of my brain and processing what was happening to my body on the other side.

The one side thought again: *You really should call 911.* But what was I supposed to say? *Is a ghost beating the crap out of me?* One thing was sure: I *really* needed to get rid of this guy on the phone.

Somehow, I managed to end the conversation and hang up the phone. I didn't know what was going on with me, so I decided I would shake it off and work through whatever it was. I shook myself, trying to clear my head. I turned toward my keyboard to work the pile of paperwork staring at me. A few minutes later, I could hardly keep my eyes open. I hadn't been so exhausted in my entire life. I thought: *If only I could close my eyes for five minutes, I would feel much better.*

Things began moving in slow motion again. I looked at the clock as I laid my head on my desk—2:11 pm. I must have fallen asleep because I woke up in a haze and wondered what I had been doing. The clock now read 3:41 pm. *Oh yeah, I was calling 911*, I thought. With my head still on the desk, I rolled it to look at the phone. My hand clumsily picked up the receiver, which fell on the desk, and I awkwardly dialed 9-1-1.

When the dispatcher answered, saying, "9-1-1, what is your emergency?" I realized I had no idea what the emergency actually was, so I lamely said, "I don't feel so good."

I heard her say, "Ma'am, can you spell your name please?" but I found out later she simply asked for my name.

Weird, I thought, but I did what I thought she asked. "B-R-E- N-D-A, C-A-S-T-E-R," I said.

The lady responded, "Brenda! This is your sister!"

I knew my sister, Denise, worked as a dispatcher for CDF, but I didn't recognize her voice.

I said, "Hiiii!" like a drunk might.

"Did you have a stroke?" she asked.

"No, I don't think so. But I don't feel right."

"I'm hanging up and getting some resources to you," she said. And the line clicked dead.

I must have dozed off again because I woke up with the phone still in my hand. I said hello a few times, but no one was there. Then I remembered talking to Denise. So, I awkwardly put the phone back in the cradle. I had just closed my eyes again when I heard a noise. Don Davis, one of my tenants, also happened to be the Chief of the Ramona Fire Department.

Inwardly, I groaned. I was too wiped out to deal with any tenant issues. I looked up from my perch on the desk and said, "Hey, Don. How are you?"

He responded, "The better question is: how are you?"

"Kinda tired right now," I said. "What can I do for you, Don?"

"How many fingers am I holding up?" he asked.

He held up two fingers.

I thought, *Seriously? Did he come all the way to the office to ask me how many fingers he was holding up?* Bizarre, but I was just too tired to care. I said, "That would be two, Don. Anything else?" I asked. "I really just need to close my eyes right now."

As I slowly turned my head, I saw Denise's husband, Carl. I said hello to Carl and wondered why on earth he was there. Then, I realized my mom was there too. *What the hell is going on here? I thought. Why is my mom here? Did Denise call a press conference?* I was too tired to care.

The next thing I knew, somebody was touching my shoulder. I looked up at a man I didn't know. I glanced behind him, and there were several other paramedics, a gurney, and all kinds of equipment. I wasn't alarmed that he was there. I knew he was coming because Denise had called them. What alarmed me was that I hadn't noticed them or all that equipment coming in.

All of a sudden, my cousin Debra was in the room as well. It seemed as if she flew into the room like a little pixie.

I thought *I didn't know Debra could fly.* She ran her hands all over my face, hot tears streaming down hers. Inwardly, I groaned. Debra worked part-time for us, and I thought something had happened. I said, "Debra, it will be all right. I can't deal with whatever it is now, but I'll take care of it when I get back tomorrow. Just use your key and lock the door. Whatever you do, do *not* call Bert!"

My dad—Bert—and his wife, Deanne, were at their timeshare in Carlsbad for the week. It was their first day of actual vacation, and I was *not* about to ruin it because of this little hiccup. I'll be back at my desk tomorrow, and everything will be fine.

"Debra, I have to go with these guys now, but I'll be back tomorrow," I said. "Whatever happened, I'll take care of it tomorrow, okay? Whatever you do, do *not* call Bert!"

Debra regarded me with the strangest expression. Then, the paramedic said something to her touched her shoulder, and Debra did a backward somersault through the air and flew away. I had to ask her about this ability when I got back.

The paramedic told me, "We must go to that gurney now."

I said okay and tried to get up, but I couldn't. I looked at him and said, "My legs won't work."

"That's okay," he said. "We'll roll you over there in the chair."

I tried using my legs to help propel the chair, but they were like rubber. I must have passed out during this because, the next thing I knew, I was on a gurney, strapped in, blanket on, and we were rolling out of my office. Time was slowing down again.

As they carried me down the steps on the gurney, I felt as though I was floating on a cloud. I was weightless.

They loaded me into the back of the ambulance. One of the paramedics joined me in the close quarters, his knee bumping against me. *These are deplorable working conditions*, I thought. *Someone should report this. But to whom? OSHA?*

The lead paramedic asked me about my name, address, medical info, etc. And then he asked, "What is your social security number?"

I had been lying with my eyes closed, enjoying this relaxation; then, my eyes flew open. "Are you trying to steal my identity?" I asked.

He laughed, "No, ma'am. That's what we use for billing."

"I've never heard of that," I said. "But okay." And I recited the number.

After that, he stopped talking. *Good*, I thought. *I can snooze a bit.* But I didn't snooze.

All I could think about was the tongue-lashing I would get from the doctor: *You don't take care of yourself, blah, blah, blah.* Then, I'd get a shot or pill or whatever to fix me up so I could go home. But then, who could I call that will come to the hospital to pick me up? My mind raced with such thoughts.

I felt the *clunk* as the ambulance's tires hit the dock at the hospital. We were there. I began bracing myself for the verbal attack I would surely be encountering as they pushed me down the hallway. I saw the fluorescent lights flying by, just like in the movies. I glanced to my left as if to elbow someone next to me, grin, and say: *Hey, do you see that?* People were all around as we made our way down the hall, but I didn't see them. I saw my dad's head floating above the blurred sea of faces, his hand reaching out and over the rest of them, reaching out to touch me.

Son of a bitch! I thought. *Debra called him!* I groaned, and then my eyes locked with my dad's, and I was filled with regret. I'd ruined my dad's vacation. I muttered my apologies to him, and then my eyes closed again.

I was convinced I'd be back home tonight and at my desk tomorrow, so his vacation was ruined for nothing. Despite my guilt about this, I couldn't open my eyes anymore. All I wanted to do was sleep. If only everybody would stop talking.

Eventually, things got quieter, and I heard a soft voice. It was the nurse, I think. Then, I heard my mom and sister Denise. They were whispering, but I knew it was them.

"I'm going to be sick," I said, fighting back an overwhelming urge to vomit. The nurse told me to hold on, and I felt something under my chin—a basin in which to expel my lunch. Then it happened again, and I eliminated the remaining contents of my stomach. Any remaining strength I had was completely sapped after that. I couldn't have stayed awake one more second if I tried.

The sounds and whispers of the others around me faded from my awareness. The last memory I had was of my sister gently removing my jewelry. I thought: *Hey, what are you doing? I like my bling!* But I was too tired to care, and Denise would keep it safe, so it was okay.

*

I woke up sometime in the middle of the night. It was dark with some obscure light. *Damn*, I thought. *I'm staying the night! I must have been more tired than I realized. I'll call someone in the morning to get me.*

Then I saw Denise, and I thought: *Why is she here? She's a 911 dispatcher and works long shifts.* "Denise," I said. "You need your rest. Go home. I'm fine. You don't need to be here."

"That's okay," she said. "Go to sleep."

But I couldn't sleep. I kept seeing things flying by me. It wasn't until much later that I realized it was my own arms and legs flailing about. I just couldn't feel them.

I fell asleep and later awoke to my cousin Mike standing over a chair his son Matt was sitting in. They were looking at me. I said hello and thought: *What the hell? Why are they here? I'll be home later.* My eyes closed again, and I drifted back to sleep.

Terrifying dreams tormented me. Then, I opened my eyes and saw Pastor Dan. Several residents at the Oak Tree Ranch belong to the Spirit of Joy Lutheran Church, and Dan was the pastor there. I had met him several times at social engagements. His mouth was moving, but I had no idea what he was saying. He looked as if he were in a funhouse mirror.

My head pressed back into the pillow, and I said, "Hey, Pastor Dan." He smiled, and my eyes closed again. My eyes opened next to my cousins, Debe, sitting next to me on my bed, and Randy, seated in a chair beside me.

I said, "Hello, dears," using the nickname we called each other. Debe said, "She knows us!"

Okay, I thought, what the hell is wrong with everyone? Why on Earth wouldn't I know them? Why do all these people keep coming here when I'll be home tomorrow?

I had been taken to Pomerado Hospital, home of the infamous

fluorescent lights. I was stabilized there and then transported to Palomar Hospital, where I would spend several weeks as their guest in the critical care unit before being transferred to a residential care facility called Villa Pomerado. Apparently, I had suffered a stroke. Not just any stroke, I'd find out later, but a *Wallenberg Syndrome* stroke. It's one that quite literally hits you on both sides of the brainstem—a "brain blowout," they call it—and affects both sides of your body. The odds of survival are grim at only 13 percent. Prospects did not look good for me. My deteriorated health didn't help matters. At my weight, I was quite a handful.

They decided to transfer me to Villa Pomerado Residential Care facility from the critical care unit at Palomar because the doctor told my dad there was nothing more they could do for me and what I needed most was to rest. I wasn't getting any rest in the critical care unit. I was hooked up to a myriad of monitors, and there were tubes everywhere. I thought it had been relatively peaceful—*arms crossed over my chest while holding a white lily* peacefully. But apparently, that wasn't the case.

Later, I heard how wild I was. If they hooked me up to something, I'd pull it out. I would rip off the catheters, IV lines, monitors, or whatever else they had on me. Alarms were going off all the time because I was never still. I would have to be restrained just to keep the IVs in me for a while. Denise said I never stopped moving and didn't think I got any rest. My hands were constantly moving, she said.

Much, much later, I asked my niece, Allison, how she had learned of my stroke. Her mom had told her. Allison called my dad, her grandpa, to find out more but was told: *All we can do is pray right now. It doesn't look good.* It wasn't until that conversation with Allison that I had no concept of how critical my situation had been.

Next I knew, I was in an ambulance for the transfer to the care facility. I had been dreaming during the ride. I heard talking in the ambulance, specifically my dad's voice. Since he was there, this ambulance seemed spacious and apparently had bench seats for additional passengers. They were whispering, and I heard my dad tell them that I was an heiress—something I would have to ask Denise about. Suddenly, my awareness departed. I could never have imagined what happened next.

Chapter Ten

Heaven

In the blink of an eye, I stood before archangel Gabriel. It was as if we were standing on a Hollywood film set. A dirt road in front of a large, sheer rock mountain went off into the mists. Gabriel was holding his massive, infamous sword.

His stature was immense, standing at least two stories high. He looked like the proverbial warrior on the paperback cover of a romance novel, the guy with long, flowing hair and massive muscles. And yet, despite his towering appearance, I felt no fear.

I could tell that his body was a façade. Around his eyes, nose, and mouth, he wore a mask that didn't quite fit. I could see the light emanating and pulsing like it was straining to be released from the minuscule cracks on the angel's face. He was, in actuality, pure light and energy.

I knew intuitively that his human-like appearance was for my benefit. Without this, a human could not comprehend and understand the reality of who he was. I understood his appearance would differ for everyone based on their understanding and beliefs.

I do not doubt that the vastness of the light that was him, if unmasked, would render us humans insane. Our minds would not comprehend. I simply knew this in my soul. I imagine this understanding is like gravity: we inherently know we won't float away.

Gabriel and I communicated, but there were no words on our lips. It was a pure, unadulterated communication of the soul. There was no misunderstanding between us because there were no words to misunderstand.

Gabriel raised his sword and told me, "You have a choice to make."

His massive sword touched the left-hand side of that rock formation. This is where events took a strange turn. Instantly, it was as if I was on the game show *Let's Make a Deal*. As the sword touched the rock, it dissolved to reveal what might be considered *Door Number One*. The molecules changed, and a rainbow of colors erupted, melting into a scene of infinite beauty.

"You can go," Gabriel said.

I recognized this place immediately. I knew it in my soul. I knew it was my home—my *real* home: Heaven. I was speechless. I had spent years of my life begging my Father in Heaven to take me *home*, and here I was, finally. The Archangel Gabriel was offering me the opportunity to come home.

This place was not a house or a building of any kind. It was a place of the spirit, of everything beautiful and holy. I was in a lush, beautiful forest with fairies floating in the air. A brook babbled nearby, and the forest floor was covered in a mossy carpet.

I could see down a path that led to my future there. A long way off, an outcropping of rocks represented future challenges awaiting me, I understood—but they were so far down the path, it hardly mattered.

I wanted to run! I wanted to run home and never look back. But my soul knew I had not finished what I came to this Earth to do.

With a tinge of sadness, I looked at Gabriel and said, "I can't go home yet. I'm not done."

He nodded his head and waved his sword. The whole scene dissolved. The gorgeous forest that was my home disappeared, and the misty rock mountain returned.

Gabriel pointed his sword at the equivalent of *Door Number Two*. Again, the giant rock dissolved into an ocean of color, and he said, "You can go back to exactly as you were."

Where the mountain range had been, a giant map now appeared. It was divided in half. Both halves were identical, like one of those "spot the differences" puzzles. It looked like a mining map, showing train tracks starting at the bottom of each side of a mountain and winding their way to the top.

I understood instantly the right side of the map displayed what was intended for my life on Earth from birth at the bottom to my physical death at the top. The tracks led through beautiful scenery. This path was smooth, with no significant bumps along the way. I intended to have a casual, stress-free life full of observing, learning, and giving. It was pretty much a no-brainer: kick back and enjoy.

I wondered: *Okay, exactly where am I on this path?* I knew it to be my path, so why didn't I see myself? Then, I looked at the left side of the map.

While the right side depicted what was intended for my life, the left side illustrated what I had experienced based on my life choices. I searched the map's left side, trying to find myself along the track. I couldn't find myself on the track in the safety of my little mining car. I guess that at some point, I had pulled the cart off the track. I wasn't in the cart or on the track; I was *behind* it, pushing it up the rocky mountain.

An accumulation of junk acquired throughout my life was piled high in the cart. I was struggling, not only because of the sheer weight of the cart and the crap I couldn't let go of, but because my route wasn't even a real road.

I recognized that my need to control my environment—to control everything— had me going about things all wrong. I was stunned at the sheer effort to reach this point— and I was only halfway up! I couldn't even see a way back to the track. I just looked at that and shook my head.

"No!" I said to the Archangel Gabriel. "I can't go back there! It is too damned hard. I absolutely can't go back to that. I can't do that anymore."

The thought alone horrified me, and I was grateful that the scene dissolved with my decision. That opportunity closed, and I dodged that bullet.

Gabriel acknowledged my choice and pointed his sword at *Door Number Three*. Again, my surroundings dissolved into the confetti rainbow, and the archangel Gabriel said, "You can let go." When I gazed into the scene, I saw an empty white space with an open door within its frame. Beyond the door, the opening revealed nothing except black. It was just black. Not the ordinary black like you might see in a dark room.

The absolute absence of light was the deepest, darkest unknown one could ever imagine. It was a void. All I could think was that not even a blind person could fathom the blackness this was. It was an empty, dead space. I knew this was my choice and where I needed to be.

Without hesitation, I walked away from Gabriel without a backward glance and stepped through that door into nothingness. There was no floor, and hands held high in complete surrender, I fell in a slow-motion roll head over heels.

I cannot say how long the fall lasted, but I had no worries or fears. I had completely surrendered to this darkness, and there was a profound freedom in my surrender. I ended up landing softly in our Creator's lap. Pure love encompassed me, and I was filled with complete joy, all-embracing euphoria, the likes of which I had never experienced. It was here in this most sacred of places that I was given the ultimate gift. My soul was cleansed and healed.

I did not see my Creator's face because my back was to him. He held me in his lap as one would hold a child. Pure delight, exhilaration, joy, and love—absolute love— encompassed my entire being.

Our Creator lovingly held me, comforting me as something I was entirely unprepared for took place. People talk about their lives *flashing before their eyes*, but it wasn't that exactly.

More accurately, I saw a review of the damage I had done to my soul throughout my life's journey. I saw it all—from decisions I made as a child until now. It was sobering, painful, and cathartic.

There was no turning from this review of my soul. I was a captive audience, both captivated and horrified by what I had lived and was now reliving. As much as it repelled me, I was unable to look away.

Yet, all the while, I was in the arms of such love. I somehow faced this with a new sense of resolve. There was *no* judgment—none whatsoever. This I knew absolutely.

No matter what you've done on this Earth, *it does not matter*— not here anyway. There is no judgment period. Some people like to believe in karma—if not good karma for those deserving of it, then bad karma for those who do horrible things—but that's about the extent of it in this life. Ultimately, we all must face the damage we've done to our souls.

The most horrific part of my experience was realizing how battered my soul was from the hatred I felt toward my ex-husband. I relived that fateful day when he walked in the door and made his big pronouncement nonchalantly.

I was stunned—not by the announcement itself or its content—but that I had been duped. I realized I had repeatedly and continually ignored my intuition and innate wisdom throughout this short union. I was a planner. I planned everything, always doing my best to account for all eventualities. I would go over and over it in my mind. Sadly, this amounted to my trying to control any given situation so that it lined up with *my plan*.

My husband's being gay and leaving me didn't exactly line up with that plan. I had planned the number of children and even the number of grandchildren I would have. I had pictured myself sitting in a rocker on my front porch with grandchildren running all around, giggling and laughing. So, what the hell? No imagining matched the actuality of life.

I had blamed Steve for everything. His admission of being gay had temporarily short-circuited my brain. I walked around in a dreamlike stupor for weeks, crying and grieving the loss of what I believed was my destiny.

I was so disoriented I often didn't know what day it was or whether it was day or night. I merely existed. There was no life. I tried to wrap my brain around what had just happened to me.

Why had my plan failed so miserably? And what were my new plans? Well, revenge. I schemed and dreamed only of making Steve pay for what he had done to me. He would suffer before he died; I would make sure of it. That had become my new life purpose. For ten years, this went on. For ten years, I *prayed* that God would strike Steve down. For ten years, I dreamed of the painful ways God would make Steve pay for what he had done.

But sitting there in our Creator's arms, reliving this most damaging experience, I realized the way I had been living was killing my soul. I clearly saw that I had been acting like a spoiled brat at that moment.

It was like a ten-year temper tantrum. Carrying that much anger and rage for so long was exhausting. I realized I could not live like this anymore. It was against my core nature. I burst into tears of gratitude and relief. I could move on now.

Don't get me wrong, I had a right to be pissed off, but my thinking about the situation had been all wrong. At that moment, I realized my rage was more for myself than for Steve. I had pushed my feelings aside and let someone else dictate my life.

At that moment, I understood that Steve would have to live with the damage he had done to his soul, just like we all do. My soul was in tatters; so horrible was the damage I had done to it—mere threads held it together. My life force was all but gone.

Now, I received the gift of witnessing the aftermath and fallout of my ten-year tantrum. I relived every bit of it. What did I see? For starters, I had trashed my body. I had made   the monumental decision to eat my emotions, putting on 120 pounds in one year. And I had been smoking like never before.

I practically lived on ibuprofen, downing thirty or more each day, pushing my already unhealthy self harder and harder. I had pushed everybody else away. Hell-bent on not feeling or dealing with anything. I had been living a half-life at best.

It was a slap in the face to see this. I saw my way wasn't so hot after all. Then, my Heavenly Father *lifted* all this from me, healing my soul and giving me new life. It was instantaneous and miraculous, like being washed clean from the inside out.

I am hard-pressed to explain this feeling of freedom and sheer joy. Unless you have experienced this for yourself, I don't know that this gift can truly ever be explained, described, or understood.

Then, I was gently set down, and I knew to start walking. I walked to the entrance of a tunnel-like opening. I didn't know where to go, but I kept walking, never looking back.

The farther I walked into the tunnel, the darker it was. Yet, I had no fear. I knew the tunnel was not dark, but my eyes had yet to adjust to its light. Walking away from the brilliance of God's heavenly light made everything else seem dark.

Then, I heard a rumble and intrinsically knew to follow it. I realized that the rumble was, in fact, prayers being offered on my behalf. They were like a beacon leading me back to my body. How long this side journey lasted, I couldn't say. Time did not even apply. I woke in what might have been the blink of an eye.

Chapter Eleven

Return to Earth

My return to Earth and my corporeal body occurred suddenly. It took me a minute, but eventually, I became aware and tried to remember what I had done. I was so tired I couldn't actually open my eyes.

What's going on? I wondered, trying to remember. Then, it came to me. I didn't remember exactly where I had heard it, but somebody had said I had a stroke. All I felt was relief that it was over. I thought: *Okay, at least that's over. I can go home now.* I tried to get up. Strong hands gripped my arms and gently but firmly pushed me back down.

I heard my dad say, "Where are you going?"

Confused and unable to open my eyes, I thought: *Isn't that obvious?* "I'm going home," I said. Once again, I attempted to get up. Once again, those arms pushed me back down.

"Surely you realize how impractical that is," my dad said.

That gave me pause, and I thought about it. Both sides of my brain chimed in.

One side said: *Let's see. I know what's happened. We're good to go, right?*

The other side said: *Um... you better listen to your dad. We've got damage reports coming in from all sectors.*

The first side responded, "I *know*, but it's over, so it's okay. We're good."

Again, I attempted to get up. Again, I was thwarted.

"Dad, I've got to go home," I said. "I've got my cats to feed."

As if on cue, I heard my little girl cat, Bell, cry. I became frantic. She needed me. I struggled to get up.

"Marian is taking care of your cats," my dad said.

"What?" I said, hardly listening. I was too busy trying to get up. Finally, I calmed down.

"Marian is taking care of your cats," he repeated.

Marian was my friend and neighbor. The cats wouldn't starve. They would be okay. I relaxed and fell asleep.

Chapter Twelve

Therapy

I don't know how long I slept, but when I woke up, I felt euphoric, as if I were the luckiest woman in the world. I had a feeling of complete bliss because my soul had been restored. I felt completely free of worry at that moment. My body still felt as though it were floating.

That euphoria lasted for some time, and I shared my good fortune of being the luckiest woman on Earth with all who would listen. I basked in it. However, the grim reality of my circumstances began crashing in on me all too soon. I slept *a lot.*

Every action I attempted took tremendous effort and left me completely exhausted. People had to feed me, which oddly felt very natural. Why wouldn't somebody feed me? Having no use of my hands seemed strange, but I didn't worry about it.

I was still too tired to open my eyes when I had my first shower since returning. They carted me around on a gurney topped with a child's wading pool. They wheeled me down to the shower room bathroom area, scrubbed me down, and hosed me off. It was like a carwash. Afterward, I felt so good, so refreshed and clean. My physical recovery was another story.

I constantly felt the sensation of lying on hard, fist-sized plastic balls that pressed into the middle of my back. I asked everyone who came in to please get them out, but no one knew what I was talking about because there was nothing there.

I would learn later that when I had the stroke, apparently, my whole body seized up. It created a series of knots in my muscles. The ones I felt at that time were in my back. The feeling of hard plastic balls constantly digging into me was my life then. I moved as little as possible so as not to aggravate the discomfort.

My left eye had to be taped shut because it wouldn't close all the way, and the cornea was drying out. My right eye was stuck looking toward my nose. When the doctors would visit, they'd ask me to follow their fingers with my eyes.

Apparently, I would move my head back and forth instead. So, they'd tell me to do it without moving my head. But I couldn't. My eyes wouldn't work like that anymore. On top of that, there was a constant *whoop-whoop* sound, as if a helicopter was perpetually landing.

I had to filter through a lot to understand what people were saying. I still had no use of my arms or legs. When the nurses put me in an inclined position, I always slid down toward the end of the bed. They had to come in and hoist me back up several times daily.

Food was problematic for a few reasons. All my food was pureed. Paralysis in the mouth and throat lends itself to choking, so cuisine of the puréed variety was the fare of the day—every day. To top it off, the food was terribly bland. I wasn't hungry, so I didn't care if I ate. Often, I wouldn't.

Another problem was talking. It was as though someone had installed an on switch in me that was motion activated. Anytime someone came into the room, my mouth would start going.

I sometimes fell asleep talking and would pick up right where I left off when I woke up. My dad set the rule that everybody had to leave when food arrived. Otherwise, I would just talk and not eat.

I just wanted to go home. One day, my dad came in, caught my one good eye, and held my chin so he knew I saw him.

He said repeatedly, "You have to eat this so you can get strong and get out of here."

Finally, it dawned on me. He was telling me *how* to get home. After that, I did my best to eat what was given to me.

One day, a feeling of despair crept into my being. I felt frustrated by not having any use of my hands. My dad was in the room and straightening things around. My sense of self-worth up to that point had been based on what I could do for others. It always had been.

That day, I realized I had nothing to give—absolutely nothing. I decided to get the cup on my tray and have a drink. My hand did not do what it was supposed to and hit the cup, causing the domino effect.

Everything on the tray was tipped over and wet. My dad turned and began laboriously picking everything up and drying it off. I felt tears welling up in my eyes.

Feeling dejected, I said, "Dad, I can't even do this." I gestured toward the tray.

He looked at me and said, "I know, Hon, but you're here. That's the important thing."

His hand swept around the room, and he said, "Nothing else matters. *You* are here."

As hopeless as the situation was, my dad helped me realize I did have some value, some kind of worth—minimal as it may have been. It was enough to keep me going. Without that, I might have given up. I might have decided it was just too hard and had them park me in a wheelchair in a corner someplace and call it a day.

I celebrated my fifty-third birthday there and asked my dad and his wife, Deanne if they would buy a giant cake for the staff. It was fun, and everyone enjoyed it. It was my little way of being of some value.

One day, a speech therapist came to visit me. She dealt with cognitive abilities, among other things. She asked if she could tell me a story. I agreed.

It went something like this:

Mr. Brown had a farm.

Mr. Brown had a wife.

Mr. Brown had a son.

Mr. Brown had a car.

Mr. Brown went to town.

When the story was finished, she asked me, "Who was the story about?"

I looked at her, and while I *knew* she had just told me a story, I had not retained one iota of the content. I was much more focused on hearing her words than what she was saying or what the words might mean. It was strange indeed, and for my life, I couldn't tell her what the story was about.

She said, "That's okay, I'll be back tomorrow."

Weird, I thought.

The next day, the speech therapist came again. Same thing: she told me Mr. Brown's story.

When she finished, she looked at me and asked again, "Who is the story about?"

With a question, I replied, "Mr. Brown?" "Good!" she exclaimed.

It seemed like the floodgates opened after that, and therapy began in earnest.

Physical therapy was the worst. The euphoric part of recovery ended abruptly. I felt all right while lying still, but the movement was another story. The therapists would start moving my left limbs up and down. The pain was unimaginable.

My eyes rolled back into my head the first time they did this. After a time, I could tell my left side was beginning to come back. I knew it wouldn't be long before the right side came back, too. *I'll be home before I know it*, I told myself.

One day, two physical therapists came to my room. This was to be my first attempt to stand. They sat me on the edge of the bed, and each one stood by my side to help. As they held me up, my feet felt like they were being impaled by large stakes.

The attack on my nervous system seemed so abrupt and brutal that there was no time to breathe. It went beyond the scream that was stuck in my throat; I felt it at the core of my being. It felt like hours, but in all reality, it was maybe a minute.

Bolts of green lightning jetted through my body with such force that I have no idea how I was upright. Finally, I was allowed back to my seated position on the bed.

"You're okay," they said, trying to reassure me. But I was not okay. I didn't think I would ever be okay again.

I don't know how often they came, but the green lightning pain would slowly subside to a dull roar when I stood. Not all systems were exactly a go. To that end, I was catheterized each morning to stimulate my stunned bladder. I'd spread 'em and put my hands up in mock surrender.

The nurse asked, "What are you doing?"

"Surrendering to the pee police," I replied. She laughed, and our daily routine began.

"Pee police," she'd announce each morning when she entered my room.

Dutifully, I'd assume the position, and this otherwise unfortunate situation took on the qualities of a tolerable routine.

My hands were the next thing we worked on. My right side hadn't perked up like my left, so my right hand didn't work. One day, one of the sweet female nurses came in with breakfast.

"Open your hand," she said. She had positioned me to sit up.

I opened my somewhat functional left hand. She placed a spoon in it.

"Close it," she said.

I did so, and she smiled.

"Enjoy your breakfast," she said and left the room.

This was new. Normally, someone came in to feed me. There was a big bowl of pureed oatmeal sitting in front of me. How hard could it be, right? Spoon in a bowl; spoon in mouth. *No problem*, I thought.

However, it was a bit more challenging than I anticipated. There was oatmeal *everywhere*. In my hair, on my gown, on my face, on the bed, on the tray, on the blankets, on and on…

The nurse came in a bit later.

"Oh goodness," she said. "Let's clean you up!"

"When do I get a shower?" I asked.

She replied, "Oh, hon, that's only Wednesday."

I'm in hell, I thought. It was Thursday.

Most meals ended up like this. Having no sense of touch made eating a bit tricky. Whenever I'd try to grab something, it was like I had a repellant on my hands, and things would fly.

111

Ice water was a particularly ruthless nemesis. *I can do it*, I thought each time I wanted a drink. The nurse probably cleaned me up and changed me seven times that day. I was determined not to call her again. But I drenched myself again, ice cubes melting on my neck.

To make matters worse, I had slid back down toward the end of the bed. *Fuck it*, I thought and closed my eyes and went to sleep. Tomorrow would be a better day. It just had to get better.

*

The days melded together, but each day brought less intense pain and the feeling I'd be home soon. There was something new every day: new limitations and obstacles to overcome.

My biggest adventure was learning how to walk with the assistance of a walker. My first objective was to make it to the bathroom. It was a slow process, but I'm happy to report I figured it out.

After that, I wanted to start writing my name. When I got better and returned to work, I'd need to be able to sign checks. My dad brought me pencils and paper to practice. I was ready to roll except for a tiny detail: Somehow, I had forgotten how to hold a pen. Weird.

So, I asked the nurse, who kindly showed me. But it didn't feel right. It was awkward and unnatural. I felt like a child learning how to use my hands for the first time. It was surreal.

I put the pencil on the paper, and *zing!* The pencil flew across the room. Good thing I had more pencils. It wasn't long before my entire stash of pencils was scattered across the room. I called the nurse, and she came and picked them up repeatedly that day.

It was worse than the ice-water debacle. Denise came to visit, and I told her of my plight. She thought thicker pencils, like kindergarten kids used, might help me readjust.

The next day, she brought big, chunky markers that my hands could more easily grasp. It wasn't easy, but I spent considerable time trying to master these monsters. When Denise came back later, she burst into laughter.

While wrangling the markers, trying to keep them in my hand, I had tagged myself and everything around me with rainbow streaks. My face, clothes, arms, hands, and work surface were covered in markers. Of course, it wasn't a shower day.

After physical therapy, I was wheeled back into my room and put back into bed. I was just getting the hang of it when, one day, a new physical therapist joined me for my walk. Instead of ending up in my room, he parked me in front of the nurse's station.

"It's almost lunch," he said. "Someone will be by to get you soon."

Stunned beyond words, I thought: *Oh my God. He's new. He has no idea I'm supposed to be in bed. He's going to be in so much trouble when they realize this.*

As if on cue, one of the certified nursing assistants came running up to me and said, "Oh, thank goodness I found you! The nurse has been looking for you!"

I knew it! I thought. *He's going to be in trouble now, for sure.*

However, this was not because I was missing from my bed. Apparently, it was my time to pee, which was now scheduled. After this quick bathroom break, she wheeled me into my room, where my bed was. We would be reunited at last! But that simply was not the case.

She wheeled me in, backed me into the space between my bed and the window, and said, "Lunch will be here in a minute."

Before I could even speak, she was gone. I panicked. *What was happening to my routine?* I thought. *I can't get into bed on my own, and I'm supposed to be there!* I was hyperventilating.

But then, I looked out the window. It was a bright, sunny day. The flowers were in bloom. A man was mowing the lawn. I could almost smell the freshly cut grass. It reminded me of another time.

Then, a butterfly flew right in front of my window and lingered there. I thought: *What a beautiful day this is.* I wondered why I ever thought I needed to be in my bed. After all, I don't live in bed when I'm home. So, I spent the day sitting up. After lunch, I practiced my writing.

That night, my sister, brother-in-law, and mom came to visit.

I asked them candidly, "When am I going home?"

I could walk about ten steps now, so I figured I was good to go.

They all started laughing.

I regarded them wordlessly, clearly disappointed.

"Oh, Brenda," my mom said. "You'll be here at least six more weeks."

"What?!"

"And even then, you'll have to go to Sharp rehab," Denise pointed out. "I heard that place is more like a boot camp than physical therapy."

I felt sick. I just wanted to go home. That night, when the lights were out and I was alone in my room, I cried. It was the first time I had cried for myself since the stroke. I was devastated. I couldn't understand what was so wrong with me. Why couldn't I go home? I did a full assessment. I thought about it for hours.

Finally, I accepted it. From the top of my head to the tip of my toes, my body was broken. Not only was my physical body brutalized, but all five senses were also severely compromised. Nothing seemed to work properly.

It was so overwhelming that I prayed. I gave thanks. I decided to be grateful instead of making demands of myself. My prayers lulled me to sleep.

Chapter Thirteen

Boot Camp

I remembered my revelation the next morning and agreed with the situation. This was for the next few weeks, so I knew I had better make the best of it. Even if it was six more weeks, the time would go by swiftly as long as I kept the right attitude and made progress.

"You're on 'bites' today," a voice said sweetly.

"Bites" were a move from pureed cuisine to tiny cut-up pieces of food. A speech therapist I had recently worked with entered the room, meeting my air of positivity.

"How does that sound?"

I couldn't believe what I was hearing. I thought to myself: *Are you kidding?* However, I hadn't eaten real food for at least a month, so I worried how that would go. She brought me Eggs Florentine.

The therapist had to hold my throat while I was eating to make sure the muscles were working properly so I could eat without choking, but I didn't care. It was the best thing I had ever eaten. It was like a world-class chef had made this dish.

Shortly after that, I was told that I was going to be moved to the inpatient section of Sharp HealthCare Physical Rehabilitation Facility. Apparently, being able to sit up by myself in a wheelchair all day and the move from pureed food to bites were signs that it was time to move on. I didn't even have to wait six more weeks.

Denise and Carl drove me over to Sharp inpatient rehab. Once there, I was wheeled in and taken to my room. After a while, I was wheeled to another building, where I was given a sonogram and x-rays to make sure I didn't have any blood clots.

After I was settled in, the physician's assistant (P.A.) said, "Okay, we're going to put you on Coumadin—a blood thinner."

"No," I said. "I'm not going on Coumadin."

My brain was still pretty slow from the stroke, so I was surprised I had the wherewithal to be so confident about this.

"Everybody who's had a stroke is on Coumadin," the P.A. said patiently.

"Well, not me," I said. "You *have* to be on it."

"No, I don't, and I won't go on it."

"Why?" she asked.

"Because I've been told that I had two blood vessels burst in my brainstem and that the bleeding might not be stopped," I said. "I've made it this far. I'm not going to bleed out in here because you want me to take Coumadin."

"Well, okay then," she said. "But you'll have to have a stimulator on your legs at night."

"That's fine," I said.

I learned what my new routine would be. I would have physical therapy, occupational therapy, and speech therapy every day. Since my insurance was with Kaiser Permanente, I would be required to do these six days a week.

I was *never* allowed to get up or down or in or out of beds and wheelchairs without assistance. An accidental fall from trying to move by myself could result in expulsion from the program.

Therapy time was therapy time end of story. There were absolutely *no* visitors during therapy time. Visitors during therapy time could result in expulsion from the program. It turned out that almost anything could result in expulsion from the program.

Lastly, I was shown all the reference information, such as how to call the nurses, order meals, and general housekeeping details.

The first day was drawing to a close. Dinner would be served shortly, I was informed. Due to my late arrival, I would get a potluck, but I was told to make out my next day's menu tonight.

"I'm still on bites, right?" I asked, a slight note of panic in my voice.

She smiled and said, "Yes, you're still on bites."

Thank God. I couldn't stand the thought of going back to puréed cuisine.

The P.A. joined me for dinner, and we discussed more of the ins and outs of Sharp Inpatient Rehab. Afterward, she told me to relax and get some rest. My intense therapy would start the next day.

118

Relax? I thought. *With a tough boot camp ahead of me? Was she kidding? Look at me. I'm overweight. I can't walk. How am I going to do this? I can't do anything.*

I feared I would fail and be sent home—a complete loser. I went to sleep, nervous about the next day. My recovery process would demand far more from me than I could have imagined.

Chapter Fourteen

Recovery

When the early-morning wakeup call arrived, the floor was buzzing with activity. Nurses, therapists, patients, food servers, and all personnel rushed about. It appeared to be quite chaotic.

However, I realized there was a perfect order to it all. Staff members took patients in shifts to the bathroom; they took vitals, served meals, and helped patients get dressed. Everyone was accounted for. Truthfully, the organization was extraordinary.

My day began with physical therapy. I figured that would be it for me, and I'd be going home later that day, considering how little I could do. It took a while for me to realize the entire point of being there was to help me actually be *able* to do something.

Liz was my lead physical therapist. She showed up first and brought an intern with her. They wheeled me down a bland hallway lined with support bars, and everyone engaged in similar exercises.

Everybody was walking or trying to, anyway. I wasn't alone. Some were holding onto the bar on the wall. Others walked with canes. Some used walkers.

Learning to stand—let alone walk—was serious business for me and required total concentration. I didn't have time to gawk at anyone else. Liz and the intern helped me stand up from the wheelchair. I grabbed onto the walker they placed in front of me. I didn't have much feeling in my legs, so they stayed close as I took a few tenuous steps with the walker.

The walker was a bust. My right foot kept knocking it sideways, almost taking me down. That only lasted two or three times before I simply said enough. I was wheeled back to my room to rest while I waited for occupational therapy to begin.

Our first session was basically about how to dress yourself— ridiculous as that sounds. I failed my first test: putting on shoes. I struggled to sit in that wheelchair as it was. Every attempt to put the shoe on only pushed me farther away from it. After a while, the occupational therapist took mercy on me.

"Stop," she said as she regarded me. "What might you do differently?"

I was puzzled. I was doing everything I could to get that shoe on. I shrugged and shook my head.

"You might try locking the wheels on the chair," she offered.

Duh, I thought. Putting my shoes on was not easy, but putting the wheelchair in Park made this daunting task a little easier. That was the end of occupational therapy for the day.

Wait, I thought. *That was it?* I had built this therapy boot camp up to be something big and scary. Did I make it a bigger deal in my mind than it really was?

Speech therapy with Louis was up next. He wheeled me into his small office. Fortunately, this was more about cognitive abilities than actual speech performance. We played word games—one of my favorite things to do. It didn't exactly feel like work. I was happy about that.

After our time was up, I was wheeled back into my room. Having been a person who was always busy before the stroke, I quickly became bored. I'm not a big T.V. watcher, so I wondered what to do. Fortunately, visitors started arriving, which kept me occupied.

My eye was finally released from having to wear a patch constantly. The downside was that my eye had become weak from not being used. The new tactic was to put a patch over the other eye for a while; the weak eye would be forced to work and become dominant once again.

Then, I'd switch the patch to the other eye. This routine seemed to go on for an eternity, and my eyes always felt tired and dry. The stubborn eye was taped shut at night since it refused to shut completely.

My daily tasks seemed to intensify, adding more responsibility for my health as the days passed. I was wheeled to a gym and had to stand and walk while holding onto parallel bars. My head was facing down so that I could see what I was doing. *Don't look down*, they'd say. That was easier said than done.

I couldn't feel my legs. Without looking down, I didn't know how I was even standing. *What was holding me up?*

The therapist put a full-length mirror at the end of the parallel bars so I could watch myself walk—and keep my head up.

What a sight! I looked terrible. I had only seen my face at the other care facility. To see a half-paralyzed face staring back at me was bizarre. I was huge. I wanted to cry but wouldn't allow myself to do that in front of everyone.

So, I just focused on my legs. Dragging my right leg behind me, I willed myself to the end. As I was exhausted, the therapist rolled me back to my room. I didn't have much feeling in my hands either. Unless I was looking at them, I couldn't do much with them.

My task for occupational therapy was to palm a penny. I was given a tray with a handful of pennies. The goal was to use my finger to drag the penny, pick it up between my thumb and forefinger one-handed, and place it in my palm. That kept me busy the entire afternoon.

When my dad and Deanne came to visit later that night, I couldn't wait to show them what I could do. I put the penny out on the tray and performed my new feat.

When the penny was firmly ensconced between my thumb and forefinger, I held it to them and triumphantly announced, "Look!"

I felt so proud of myself. Puzzled, they looked at each other, then turned to me and said with a smile, "Wow! That's great!"

At the time, being able to pick up a penny felt monumental. However, one-handed penny-picking wouldn't keep me occupied for long. I practiced picking up pennies and writing until I couldn't stand it.

I mentioned my boredom to my speech therapist, Louis. He came to my rescue and gave me *homework*. This included a plethora of word and logic games. They became my new passion. Whenever I was alone, I would do my homework.

Denise brought a picture of my two kitties to put by my bedside. It wasn't so bad. The staff was very friendly too. Yet I just wanted to go home. Denise was also the one who would tell me to suck it up when things got tough. She was right. What else could I do?

In life, there aren't exactly any do-overs. No matter how much I wished I had done things differently, I just had to suck it up, accept what had happened, and move on. I would be tested here, simple. Life was full of such tests.

My physical therapist, Liz, handed me some papers.

"I found this article on the type of stroke you had," she said. "It's called a Wallenberg Syndrome Stroke."

She explained it occurs on both sides of the brain stem. She said only 13 percent of people who have this type of stroke survive, probably because the area damaged controls automatic features like breathing and swallowing.

Reading wasn't easy for me, so I gave the article to my dad when he came in. The 13 percent survival rate didn't mean much to me then. Only later would I realize how phenomenal it was that I was still alive.

Later that week, Liz took me to the gym for a session. My goal for the day was to stand unassisted. I knew my legs would hold me because I had seen it myself, but I could not do it that day. *Why can't I do it?* I could stand up but would immediately fall back into the chair.

Up, down, up, down; on and on it went. I could not maintain balance to save my life. It was such a simple task, yet I couldn't do it. It was infuriating. I felt like I was going to crack from frustration. I sat in my chair, holding my hands over my eyes and trying to be strong.

"I'll be right back," Liz said, excusing herself.

I knew any second I might start screaming. My frustration was boiling into rage. I hated myself for being in this ridiculous situation. *Why was this happening to me? Why can't I stand? I hate this!*

Envenomed thoughts rushed through me. I was breathing hard, trying to contain my fury, my pain, and my loss. I knew if I had started screaming, I would never stop. Did I care? I was pondering that thought, and right before I was about to vocally unleash my rage, Liz reappeared.

"Brenda, I want to introduce you to someone."

Are you freaking kidding me? I thought. *At a time like this? I'm about to snap!*

"Brenda," she said in a soothing tone. "This is Nick."

I plastered a fake smile, looked up, and gritted my teeth. "Nice to meet you."

"Nick had a Wallenberg Syndrome Stroke two weeks before you did."

My head snapped up at those words, and I looked her in the eye. She acknowledged with a nod of her head. I regarded Nick. He was older than me, but—more importantly—he could walk. He didn't look like much had happened to him at all.

Wow, I thought. *If that old geezer can do it, so can I!*

That day was a game-changer for me.

Chapter Fifteen

Hard Work

Sometimes during the day, I would sit on my bed and look out the window. I had a view of the courtyard and could see the other patients in the stroke recovery program walking the obstacle course of stairs and ramps. I'd watch them with longing, wishing I could do what they did. Little did I know, I'd be eating my words soon enough.

When it was finally my turn for the obstacle course, I learned those beautiful moments of regained mobility came from hard work. Walking backward and forward on different surfaces— grass, textured concrete, gravel—was harder than I could have imagined.

Before the stroke, I never worried about or even gave much thought to where my foot was placed. I had taken the art of walking for granted. There was a lesson in there, somewhere.

My sister, Debbie, and her daughter, Allison, visited me from Florida. They bought me an iPad, which changed my world. I didn't think I'd be able to use it because I still could not pick up a phone and dial it, but they bought a gorilla-proof case for the iPad. This way, it wouldn't break when I'd inevitably drop it.

I didn't know it then, but I was far from returning to my office computer. At the time, I was confident that when I got out, I'd immediately be back at my desk. That was a given in my mind. The reality, however, would be a bit different.

My dad always asked if there was anything he could bring me. So, I took him up on it and asked for the old calculator from my desk at the office. It didn't work properly, but that didn't matter. I wanted to practice my ten-key finger movements.

I imagined my fingers moving over the keys. I told myself *I'd be zooming along in no time, ninety miles an hour again, handling work*. I wanted to be ready. However, when I pulled out that ten-key to practice, my well-trained fingers simply couldn't do it— not anymore.

I was devastated and in tears when the occupational therapist arrived. Crying, I explained what had happened and realized I wouldn't return to work anytime soon. She counseled that I would need to share this new understanding with my dad.

When my dad and Deanne arrived that evening, we went to a small room and shut the door. Bawling, I broke the news to them. I felt useless.

"I'm so sorry," I said.

No other words came to mind. No other words would suffice. Work had been my sole identity for so many years. Now what? What was there for me? How could I just leave my dad to deal with everything? *I am scum*, I thought.

They must have been surprised at the fierceness of my tears

because they began making assurances that couldn't have been true. Whatever the case, it was done. I had admitted to myself, as much to them, the sad truth of the matter. When they left, I put the calculator away, never again to revisit that traitor.

*

Before long, I was mastering many aspects of my daily routine, such as getting dressed for the day. That part had always been made easy because I asked my sister Debbie to get my clothes and put them in a bag hooked on the end of the bed. A brilliant solution to my morning struggles! And yet, this shortcut was short-lived.

As I was preparing to get dressed, a nurse took my prepared bag of clothes out of my hands and tossed it across the bed where I couldn't reach it. Then, she walked out of the room as if nothing had happened. I called after her.

"I have physical therapy first thing this morning!" I shouted.

She paid no attention to me. When Liz and her intern came in for physical therapy, they were not happy with me.

"Why are you not dressed?" Liz demanded.

I didn't blame her for being irritated; I was annoyed, too. I pointed to the bag of clothes on the bed.

"Ask the nurse," I said. "She tossed my clothes where I couldn't reach them."

Liz left to talk to the nurse while the intern helped me dress. This put a kink in the schedule. Apparently, the nurse had the wrong bed; occupational therapy was scheduled to watch the girl next door get dressed. My turn would be the following day.

*

The overall gait of a survivor of a Wallenberg Syndrome stroke was apparently unique because I was asked if I'd agree to be filmed for educational purposes. Since the survival rate was so rare, it was hard to get first-hand observations.

By now, I had mastered getting out of my wheelchair, standing, and walking short distances. *Lights, camera, action!* The filming commenced. I stood up as the camera started rolling, but before I could take a step, plop. I fell right back in the chair.

"Cut!" I cried. "Take two!"

They laughed and said it was all on film.

What? I thought. *Oh my God!* Embarrassed and mortified at my lack of standing ability, I tried again, but to the same effect: *plop!*

By now, we were all laughing, which made it even more challenging, but eventually, I made it up and started walking. And we made our educational video.

*

One aspect of my recovery I wasn't crazy about was how many pills I had to take. I was taking a *lot* of pills. I mentioned this to Louis one day.

"I don't even know what they're all for," I said.

130

He seemed surprised, "You certainly have a right to know what your medications are for."

"I do?"

"Of course you do," he said. "All you have to do is ask the nurse."

I had to ask the nurse a few times, but eventually, the P.A. came in to go over the medications with me. One of the medications they mentioned was a seizure medication.

I looked at her with confusion and said, "I have seizures?"

"Don't you?"

"Not that I know of," I said nervously. "Do I have them here and just don't know it?"

"No, you haven't had a seizure here," she said, reviewing my chart. "I'll have to find out exactly why you're on this."

It turned out that no one knew. It appears I was prescribed this drug while in the critical care unit for preemptive measures, presumably. Unfortunately, it was a narcotic, so I couldn't just stop taking it. They had to wean me off it.

This made me question everything that had been prescribed for me. I had them tell me what each medication was for. I would have cut them all if it had been up to me, but I agreed to keep taking what the P.A. felt was necessary.

*

It wasn't long before I was to start operating my wheelchair by myself. My days as a mere passenger were coming to an end. It was liberating in many ways, but there was a problem: I still didn't have much feeling in my hands.

I was not confident enough to put them near the moving metal spokes. I could break my fingers and not even know it. It was awkward, but that's how it rolled—no pun intended. Eventually, I figured it out and kept my fingers intact.

Now that I had regained a little independence, I signed up for recreational therapy. The program offered various activities, including crafts, exercise, gardening, and multiple games. I participated in everything I could to keep myself busy and pass the time.

One day at breakfast, I awoke to the food tray being shoved under my chin. My bed had not been raised to a proper seating position, and there was no way I could get my arms up and over to even attempt to eat. I was not a happy camper. I felt humiliated.

When the P.A. came in for her regular visit, I asked if I could eat sitting on the side of the bed from now on.

"No," she said, "it's not allowed."

I explained what happened and told her if they ever did that again, I would find a way to send the tray crashing to the floor. That was the last meal I ate in that bed. The next day, I was helped into my wheelchair and dined from the comfort of that for the rest of my stay.

Meanwhile, the days dragged on. My stay was scheduled for six to eight weeks, and I was barely halfway there. My insurance coverage was contingent upon continual, significant progress within a set of parameters. As with my stay at the care facility, I had zoomed to the top of those parameters. So, my stay would end soon.

And yet, several things would have to happen before I could be released. I had already made good progress in transferring from a wheelchair onto a chair into a bed, and so on, and a wheelchair was ordered for me to take home. But I would also have to demonstrate that I could get myself off the ground in a fall.

My family and other caregivers would need to learn how to properly support me. Next, a meeting would be held with medical personnel, therapists, family, friends, and me to discuss my ongoing care. It was going to be a busy few weeks.

Getting up off the floor was not fun, nor was it easy. My whole body often hurt, so even these drills were difficult. I had to sit at the end of the raised mat, ease my way to the floor, and lie down on my back, simulating a fall. Then, I had to turn myself over, get on my knees, crawl to the edge of the mat, and pull myself up.

This took me a while to figure out because my right side still wasn't fully working. At times, I couldn't remember which way to turn and ended up spinning around, first one way, then the other. It was ridiculous and painful.

My friend Marian was there, watching this latest feat of mine. I got up on the mat and was puffing and breathing hard when, to my disbelief, I heard her ask Liz if she could see that again.

Seriously? I thought. I was dumbfounded. I looked at Liz as if to say: *No way.*

But Liz shook her head and said, "Nope. She's right. Let's see that one more time."

I believe an f-bomb left my lips as I lowered myself to the mat for my encore. Perhaps most humiliating, another condition of my release was a performance of my showering abilities—and everyone was to watch! I couldn't believe it. I argued with my occupational therapist until I was blue in the face, but apparently, it was non-negotiable.

"Then don't go home," he said bluntly. The humiliation never seemed to stop.

I had always been a fairly modest person, but experiences like a naked shower performance have a way of changing all that. Naked as a jaybird, I turned the water on and did my thing while my clothed audience stood and watched. This mortifying experience seemed to last forever.

A few days later, a new speech therapist specializing in throats came in. I graduated up to regular foods—with a few exceptions— but I was monitored just as at the care facility.

She held my throat while I ate to ensure the throat muscles did what they were supposed to. If you've never had someone hold your throat while eating, it's as awkward as you might imagine. Fortunately, this chapter of my life was coming to an end.

Chapter Sixteen

Release

On one of my last few days at the Sharp facility, my dad came and wheeled me out to the courtyard for our visit. It was a beautiful day. As part of my exit package, I was to meet with a neuropsychologist after lunch that day.

When the food service lady came and delivered my lunch, I thanked her wholeheartedly, feeling warm and grateful. My dad lifted the lid and revealed a beautiful salad.

I looked at it and sadly told my dad, "That's not mine."

I love salad, even though I hadn't eaten any in what felt like an eternity. Unfortunately, lettuce was now a choking hazard.

"Well, they brought it, so it must be okay," my dad said as he cut it up.

I looked at the salad longingly, uncertain if I should even attempt to eat it. But before I made that decision, the food service lady came back running.

"I knew it," I said, "It's not mine, is it?"

She shook her head no.

"Sorry," she said. "I have to take it back."

Oh well, I thought. I would have a salad some other day.

135

My dad left after lunch, and I met with the neuropsychologist. We discussed everything from the stroke itself to the obstacles I still had to overcome. We must have talked for hours. Finally, the moment I had been waiting for arrived, she asked me if I had any questions. As a matter of fact, I did.

I hadn't really discussed it with anyone, partly because it was so difficult to describe, partly because I thought I was going crazy.

"Why is it that I can't stop talking?" I asked. "I know I'm doing it, but I can't stop. It's like I hear two voices inside my head: One just keeps talking, even after the other says 'it's time to stop talking...'"

Talk, talk, talk.

 "It's time to stop talking now."

Talk, talk, talk.

 "For the love of God, *SHUT UP!*"

"It never ends," I said.

She explained that a part in the back of the brain sends a signal to the front of the brain, saying when it's appropriate to stop talking. The stroke damaged that part of the brain, so it's sending the signal but missing its mark.

"Most people don't actually hear that happening, though," she said.

Lucky me, I thought. However, I was glad to know I hadn't become schizophrenic as I had secretly feared.

*

Finally, the day came when I could go home. It had been a long time coming. I just wanted to be alone with my cats. All I could think of was petting my little girl, Bell, and luxuriating in her soft fur. I was so close to realizing that dream!

There was no fanfare. I made my exit in my wheelchair. I managed to get in the car, and the wheelchair was stowed in the back. My trusty driver, Denise, and her husband, Carl, and I headed out into the wild blue yonder.

We stopped at Taco Bell and treated ourselves to burritos. Then, we headed for home. My beloved cats would soon be in my arms, and I would have my life back. If only it had been that easy.

Denise parked the car in the garage, and Carl helped me inside. Denise and Carl had been busy. Grab bars had been installed on the door from the garage, in the laundry room, and in my toilet area.

Suction bars had been attached to my shower; a shower chair was set up and ready to be used. Rugs and trip hazards were removed. They had worked their asses off, going so far as to de-smoke my home and car. I couldn't thank them enough.

The room erupted in applause when I walked through the hall to the den. So many people were there to welcome me home. I thought applauding me for walking in the door was weird. It was nice that they had come, but I just wanted to be with my cats, who I imagined were freaked out with so many people around.

The visit was sweet but short-lived. Everyone had left except Megan. I couldn't live alone, and my cousin Margaret's eldest daughter was home from college for the summer. She would stay with me, help me, and take me to the next phase of therapy—a day treatment program at Sharp's medical center.

I would have the entire weekend before this new adventure began. I told Megan I would be in my room with my cats. But to my dismay, they didn't come when called. They were not as thrilled to see me as I was to see them.

I knew they were hiding in my closet, and I decided to go to them if they didn't come. I made my way out and told Megan not to panic if she saw me on the floor.

I was getting out of the wheelchair and crawling into the closet to see them. That was a bit harder than expected, but I did it without hurting myself. My legs wouldn't move into a crawling position, so I dragged my body into the closet.

Once inside, I said, "I know you're in here."

Immediately, Big T started purring. I smiled. He came out and let me touch him for about a milli-second and then disappeared out the closet door. *That little shit*, I thought. Bell, always afraid, remained silent. Her whereabouts remained a mystery.

I managed to turn myself around to get out of the closet and was surprised to see my shoes and socks. Apparently, I had dragged them off my feet without even noticing. The cats would come out at night and sniff me, but if I tried to touch them, they'd scurry away.

I was actually a bit afraid to touch them. I didn't want to hurt them by accident. Just when I thought I had a secure hold on something, I'd drop it. I would barely hold something and break it. My cats hated the wheelchair from day one. It would be a while before my fur-luxuriating day would come.

I had a whole weekend ahead of me without anybody telling me what to do. I couldn't wait. I didn't want to see anybody. In fact, the thought terrified me. Yet, I couldn't help feeling a little lonely. During recovery, I had a constant stream of visitors to the facilities.

That had all but dried up now that I was home. People went back to their lives. I did enjoy that first weekend getting used to my home again. Yet, Monday would be here all too soon. And come it did. The next phase of my life in Sharp's outpatient Community Re-Entry Program (CREP) was about to begin.

Chapter Seventeen

Miss Independent

Most days, I woke up early. Megan would wheel me to the shower and make sure I was seated safely before leaving me to wash myself. When finished, I'd wrap the towel and robe around myself and call her.

Then, she'd made sure I got safely back into the wheelchair. At this point, I would wheel over to my vanity area where my clothes were laid out, dry off, dress myself, and brush my hair. Then, Megan would wheel me to the breakfast table. She usually made oatmeal and fixed me a lunch to go.

She'd help me into the car, load that heavy wheelchair, and off we'd go. It took about an hour to get to the treatment center. She'd ensure I made it inside, then leave me with staff for six hours.

The treatment facility was a place to help people integrate back into society. It was there to help me learn how to maneuver in the world with my abilities.

The first day in, I asked what the acronym CRAP stood for—mishearing the *e* as an *a*. I was relieved to know my program was CREP and not CRAP. It stood for Community Re-Entry Program.

It was the same center where I had been an inpatient guest, just on the other side of the building. Occasionally, I'd see people I had come to know during my previous stay. I also had physical therapy, occupational therapy, and speech therapy there.

In speech therapy, I was suggested to get an app for my iPad that was like a digital parrot. It was a game that repeated everything I said. At first, I didn't understand. Everything it said came back slurred and distorted.

"Why does it do that?" I asked.

"It's repeating what you're saying," the therapist told me.

"What?"

It took me a few minutes to realize that this entire time—starting from when I had the stroke up until now—I was slurring my words.

In my mind—and to my ears—my speech was impeccable, unchanged, the same as it had always been. The sympathetic looks and requests to repeat what I said all started to make sense.

Knowing my throat and tongue were paralyzed, it should have dawned on me sooner that my speech was impaired in some fashion. *Why didn't I hear it?* I wondered. *Why didn't I know that?*

I quickly caught on to the groove of therapy. Monday mornings were for community meetings, during which one of the staff members would facilitate while outpatient members talked about what was happening with us.

There was a young man with a wife and young children at home sitting next to me the first day. He was recovering from a second stroke. He mentioned that he didn't like to be touched.

Unable to resist, I cried out, "Watch this!"

I slowly moved my finger toward him and then did it. I touched him on the arm. We all burst out laughing, even he.

There were people from all walks of life, from different age groups, and from various causes of brain injuries. Everyone had something, and no two cases were alike. Some were unable to communicate whatsoever. It worked out for me since I couldn't stop talking to save my life.

One morning, while getting dressed at home, I decided to start wearing makeup and jewelry again. Given the lack of feeling in my hands, this was quite the trick for me to accomplish.

As hard as I tried, my hands didn't exactly do as I asked. Time was running short, and I needed to leave for therapy. *I'll just finish it with some bright red lipstick*—lip stain, to be exact. I would look bright and cheery.

Have you ever seen one of those impeccably dressed old ladies but then notice those lips gone awry? That's what stared back at me in the mirror. *Oh my God*, I thought. How did that happen? The more I tried to fix it, the worse it got.

I did my best to wipe it off, but the lip stain doesn't exactly wipe off. I had no time left to get ready, and Megan hadn't said anything, so I must have done okay. Once there, I saw Liz, my old physical therapist, wheeling a new patient down the hall.

I smiled, waved, and enthusiastically said, "Look! I'm wearing makeup!"

Her smile was enormous.

"Yes," she said. "I see that."

The look on her face told me everything.

Toward the end of the day treatment program, I was asked to do a presentation. The topic I chose was quilting. I put together a slide presentation—my first ever— and brought samples of quilts to share. It went pretty well, and I was surprised to be asked by Wendy, a recreational therapist, for a donation.

I would go on to make an annual quilt to be donated to the silent auction benefiting the children's hospital nearby in San Diego. The days seemed to drag on until my release date from the day the treatment program was scheduled. Then, I would go back to my life for real. I would be on my own again.

The occupational therapist came to do a home inspection to determine whether I could, in fact, live alone. She asked me endless questions about what I would do in certain situations. Apparently, I passed.

She announced her determination in front of witnesses, who were probably there to ensure I wasn't lying about my independent status: "I see no reason why you can't live alone."

Inside, I screamed, *Hallelujah!*

When she left, the door clicking behind her, I thrust my hand out, finger pointed toward the door, and announced, "Everybody out!"

I told Megan she could get her stuff later, but everybody had to go. She gathered her things, and I was alone. I sighed, free at last. The silence was beautiful. I was a free woman again.

And then, as if my bladder conspired against me, I had to go the bathroom. I no longer had anyone's assistance, so I wheeled myself there. *Uh-oh*. I might have been a bit hasty sending everyone away. Wheeling myself around on the carpet was really hard. I got what I asked for, though. Miss Independent. There wasn't much I could do. I would have to suck it up—again.

I was excited to be home alone. The next day, showered and dressed, I made my way to my chair. I felt happy and anticipatory for this fantastic day to unfold. After a few minutes, I thought, *Now what?*

Chapter Eighteen

Settling In

Settling back into my life following such a major health crisis was quite an adjustment. The days, weeks, months, and years that followed still left me feeling lost. I went through the entire program and performed everything necessary to get out, but in all reality, I was pretty much dropped off at my house and told I was good to go.

The truth is, I wasn't. I had survived this catastrophe, but that was about it. What would I do? How was I supposed to go forward? The days turned to weeks, weeks turned to months, and I still felt lost.

However, I was walking again. I still had the wheelchair, but I used it mostly for balance. I pushed it while walking around the house. It was most helpful for me to carry things from one place to another. I knew it would have to go eventually, but was afraid to turn it in.

All kinds of *what-ifs* crept into my mind. In fact, I had tremendous fear. I had been told for months about the things I could and could not do—not to mention the things I learned on my own that nobody could have guessed would pose problems.

In the care center, I virtually had zero say in my own life. Now that I was home, I lived in fear that any wrong move on my part would result in someone determining I was not fit to live alone and that I would be moved to a facility once more against my will.

I was struggling physically, mentally, and emotionally. One thing, though, my ever-loving Heavenly Creator kickstarted my intuition—and I started listening.

One day, while sitting in my wheelchair at the table, my gut told me to get LifeLock, an identity protection service. So, I followed through and got it all set up. Someone attempted to steal my identity within two short weeks of my enrollment. *Holy cow*, I thought. The phone calls started rolling in.

"Is this you?"

"Did you open this account?"

"Did you authorize this charge?"

I couldn't believe it. I offered the same amazed answer each time, "Of course not. I'm sitting here in this wheelchair."

The thief was opening new accounts in my name. This was bad and could have been financially devastating had I not signed up for LifeLock. I had to send letters to credit reporting agencies, file police reports, and fill out tons of paperwork, but at least I had LifeLock guiding me every step of the way and shutting down all suspicious activity. It was unreal how quickly whoever did this moved. Someone even tried to get a mortgage in my name.

I had taken over paying my own bills by now, and it was slow going. I was grateful I didn't have many. Writing checks was a challenging task for me. Writing that small was one thing, but numbers were particularly difficult.

I decided I needed to walk longer distances. I *had* to return to work, and movement seemed the quickest way to get there. I asked my neighbor Marian if she would join me in my new quest for better health.

Even though she had tremendous pain in her knees, she agreed to walk with me around the cul-de-sac. My balance sucked, and her knees were too painful, so, unfortunately, this was short-lived. I started doing laps around the inside of my house, pushing that wheelchair around and around.

Putting on my shoes was probably the worst part. I had so much pain in my body. It was a twenty-to-thirty-minute ordeal each day to get those shoes on, my right foot not acquiescing to the bending action required. I was frustrated to the point of tears some days. There were times I just wanted to scream *fuck it!*

Then, I got a letter from my former brother-in-law, Don.

I will never forget his words: "I guess you're getting used to your new normal."

What? I thought. *No way is this ever going to be normal for me— ever!* I was determined to get strong. I *would* get back to work. *Screw it! I'm going to start walking down the street by myself. I can do it!* And so, I recommitted.

I got myself dressed, put on those damned shoes, and went out the front door. I walked down the two steps and went to the end of the driveway—about ten steps. Then, I remembered I had to go back too. I turned around, reversing my course, and made it to my chair and collapsed.

That little workout was exhausting. It wasn't just the physical movement that was tiring; it was the mental exhaustion, too. You don't think about how to walk after you're a kid. But, after the stroke, I had to relearn all these things that had once been automatic.

It required intense concentration. I was tired and slept a *lot*. I would take naps each day, sometimes up to five or six hours, depending on what I had done that day. Each day on my new walking regimen, I would take a few more steps to stay in a straight line. It didn't work out so well. I probably looked like a drunk weaving along the street. I will work on that next.

A friend measured my route in her car. By that time, I was doing just over a mile each day. I felt proud of myself. I imagined walking all the way to the office in short order. I could see myself back at my desk, living my normal life again. And then, my world, quite literally, went sideways.

I walked in the door after my walk, and *wham! What the hell just happened?* I asked myself. I fell sideways and clung to the wall, holding on for dear life. I made my way to a chair. The room spun. My eyes bounced around seemingly of their own volition. I stayed there the rest of the day. At some point, I called my doctor's office.

"Do I have a neurologist?" I asked.

She laughed.

"No . . . why would you need one?" the receptionist asked.

"Well, I had a stroke, and I was doing good. But now I'm not."

"Oh," she said, more serious now. "Yes, you do need one."

So, I was assigned a neurologist, and an appointment was made. My balance was worse than ever. The specialist doubled the dosage of my blood pressure medication, and that's when the odyssey began for a solution to my relapse.

My friend Debbie—God love her—was by my side, taking me to test after test, doctor after doctor, as each new medicine seemed to have problematic side effects. My hopes to be back at work were on the back burner now. I felt so depressed. I couldn't do shit.

And then, my eyes. My poor eyes began to feel that fine-grade sandpaper had been placed in the lids, scraping and rubbing constantly. It was painful, and no amount of lubrication made it subside. There were times I wanted to scream, but if I had started, I wouldn't have stopped. At times, I wanted to rip my eyes out. The irritation lasted for months.

After getting dressed each day, I would sit there in that chair and had nothing to look forward to—only a nebulous hope that this would be resolved one day. I would wait for the phone to ring, for someone to take me to the store, or for the food delivery man to ring the doorbell.

That was pretty much my life. As the days rolled by, despair crept in. The first anniversary of the stroke had come, and I felt this

149

weird obligation to write a letter or email to all the people who had sent cards or letters and let them know how I was doing.

But what would I say? I thought my six-month letter was fairly upbeat, but this one?

Hello everyone. Thank you for all your good wishes and prayers. I'm so sorry they were wasted on such a loser.

At least, that's what I wanted to write.

Despondent was the only word that came to mind to describe how I was feeling. *What on Earth could I possibly say?* I wondered. *Should I even write the letter?* Nothing was going well. I sat there in silence and heard a soft voice speak to me. It was a voice I had heard many times over the years.

"What were you doing last year?" Hmmm, what *was* I doing last year?

Oh yeah, I was lying out in a kind of coma state. With that in mind, I realized I *was* doing much better—at least better than that! What was I doing in June of last year?

Wait—that's right: I was learning to feed myself again. Visions of the oatmeal catastrophe came front and center. *Well, geez*, I thought. *I am doing way better than that!* At least I could feed myself now.

I went through the months, one by one, comparing them to how I was now. I saw very clearly what I had done. I had climbed the stairs, made it to the top, and dropped back one measly step. That's all I was focusing on.

Never mind all I had gained and accomplished; I was letting this little loss capture all my attention. The second I realized my error, I was *grateful* for everything in my life! It overflowed my entire being and my letter to those who prayed for me, which took on this new light instead of being negative.

I was happy again and relieved that something else would be coming along. I didn't know what that would be, but I'd know when it came. I'm generally not one to simply sit still and wait, so I started looking. I grabbed my trusty iPad and started searching— though I did not know for what. And then, many serendipitous opportunities arose.

For starters, I received an email from my long-time friend, Susan. In it, she mentioned a medical intuitive. Why hadn't I thought of that? My search now had a purpose. Finding the right one took a few days, but one stood out. I dialed the number, left my info, and waited.

Brian from E Healing Solutions returned my call. After a few phone sessions, I bent over and tied my shoes like a pro. My balance seemed to definitely be on the mend. I could walk longer without needing to sit, so I could actually go to the store. My eyes were relieved from the scratchy pain.

A lot of positive physical changes were made to my body. To me, this all was a miracle! Brian even offered to keep working with me for as long as I needed without additional compensation. But— like with most things in my life—my intuition told me I was done with Brian's work. It was time for me to move on.

Something was coming along that would move me to where I needed to be next. I knew it. I was at a quilt retreat— thanks to my friend Debbie—and a girl came in, gushing about this amazing thing she had just done.

She had gone to a girl who did energy work and helped to release trapped emotions. It was called the *Emotion Code*. I knew it was the next right thing for me when I heard it. I made the appointment, and it started.

It was truly beneficial. I found it so helpful that I later became certified in the Emotion Code and the next level, the Body Code. Just as before, my time with the energy worker would be ending as something new was headed my way. I never could have dreamed of the opportunity that came next.

She gave me the card of a chiropractor and said, "I think this guy can help you."

The name on the card was Michael C. O'Dell, DC. I filled out his online intake sheet and arranged a ride to see him. I will never forget my first visit. I was still slow on the uptake, and he handed me an iPad set to a sign-in page with a keypad, front and center. I dimly looked at it and then at him.

Then he said in a loud whisper, "3-7-4-2."

It took me a minute, but I understood the last four digits of my phone number was the code to sign in.

At this point, I still relied heavily on a cane to walk and did so in a hunched-over position to maintain my balance. I'll be honest: sitting there, I didn't think this guy could help me. But it did feel right to be there. *We'll see.*

He might have regretted his decision to treat me a few times. He would press on my back to make an adjustment. The pain, at times, was immediate.

With no real filters, I would moan loudly in agony and jokingly shout out to my sister, who had brought me there, "Denise! You're a witness!"

It seems like my appointment times were shifted to the last appointment of the day after that. I moved in a positive direction, slowly improving, and then a new series of synchronicities happened. Dr. O'Dell slid a card across the counter while I checked out.

"You should see this guy," he said.

The card was for a personal trainer.

"Yeah, right," I said as I slid the card back.

Are you kidding? I thought. *I can barely walk.*

He did this on more than one occasion. I finally just took the card home, thinking I'd never call the guy. At the same time, while sitting in my chair one day, I received an email from Hay House with a video from Susan Pierce-Thompson about Bright Line Eating. It was interesting and really made sense.

There were three videos in the series. The last one revealed how much this online boot camp would cost. At $997 (at the time), I almost fell over and instantly said a resounding no! I closed that iPad!

I can do this myself, I thought, and I tried to figure it out with the chicken scratch notes I had taken. I was frustrated. Then, a few days later, a fourth video addressed my reservations and questions. Was Susan Pierce-Thompson a mind reader?

I mentioned this program to my friend Kim, who had been taking me to see Dr. O'Dell, and Dr. O'Dell gave her the same "Anthony trainer guy card." Both of us agreed the Bright Line program was way too much money. By the end of that fourth video, I had decided it would be worth it. It was money-back guaranteed, and what did I have to lose but weight or $997?

I filled out the form and confidently hit the Send button. And then, panic set in. What had I done? I had pretty much just committed to giving up all types of flour and all types of sugar—for life! What had I been thinking? I started hyperventilating at my foolish decision. I texted Kim with my oh-my-God moment.

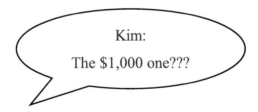

Kim:
The $1,000 one???

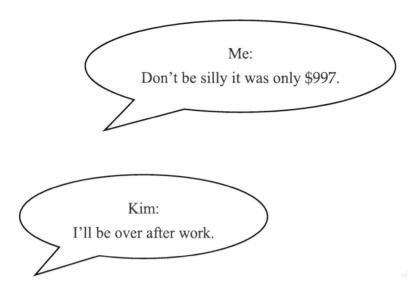

Me:
Don't be silly it was only $997.

Kim:
I'll be over after work.

The first email arrived with instructions on how to get geared up for the upcoming boot camp. Kim came, and we shared a meal while going over the crazy journey I had embarked on. Waves of panic were still present but subsided. The next day, I jumped into action before pictures were taken.

Whoa. Did I really look that big? I mean, I *had* slimmed down to a svelte 263 pounds at this point, but my appearance was worse than I had imagined. The image of me was a blow to the ego, and I took the day off!

The next day, I was to eliminate everything that listed flour or sugar within the first three ingredients. I gave this *food* away. Imagine my surprise when my enormous pantry, packed to overflowing, was pretty much bare. I did a massive cull of the freezer as well. In the end, it was almost empty.

Wow, really?

In frustration, I poured myself a cup of coffee and said out loud, quite vehemently, "I can't have coffee without sugar!"

"Wow," I heard myself say, and responded, "Well, Brenda, I guess if you say you can't, I guess you just can't."

This was a turning point for me, and I understood the real power of words. I formulated a plan. Instead of two large teaspoons of sugar, I would cut to one the first day, and each day after that, I would cut that by half until no sugar was added to my coffee. Within a week, the last of my sugar was out of my house. I was ready to start this boot camp.

Honestly, I didn't have much support from my family, who, I'm sure, thought this was just another of my hare-brained ideas. So, I just stopped talking about it with them. I knew I could do this.

I was sitting at my table, contemplating things and looking around online, when a voice inside me said: *Call Anthony.*

What? That trainer guy?

"Okay," I said aloud, "When Kim gets home, I'll see if she can give me a ride."

Thinking the matter settled, I carried on with what I was doing. The voice returned. *Call Anthony.*

It didn't take much to exasperate me those days, so I said a bit louder, "Okay! When Kim gets home, I will!"

Before I could even get back to my iPad, the loud and commanding voice said: *CALL ANTHONY NOW!*

"FINE!" I shouted back, grabbed his business card, and dialed the phone.

He answered. I was blunt and had an attitude going on. I was irritated and didn't want to call him, *and* I didn't think he could help me.

At the end of my bitter spiel, I asked, "So, do you think you can do anything for me?"

He said, "Yes, I think I can help you."

I didn't believe him, but I made the appointment. A few days later, Kim took me to the scheduled meeting. I was asked to walk, sit down, stand up, and perform similar movements. After my various feats of minimal exercise, he actually said he could help me.

The Bright Line Eating program started within days, *and* I had a personal trainer. One thing this eating program required was to plan and track my food. I had *no* idea how often my hand went to my mouth each day until I became conscious of what I was eating. It was crazy.

I always thought: *Well, I'm eating lettuce; for God's sake, how can I gain all this weight?* The tracking helped me realize I wasn't only eating lettuce. I was snacking on little things all day long. It was eye-opening, to say the least.

Then, the personal training began. To start, he asked me to use the foam roller. I had to get my girth on the ground, which was not an easy feat, lay my chunky thighs on this hunk of foams, and glide over it.

157

The foam roller pressed deeply into my body. The pain was unbearable. I lasted only a few seconds. I rolled from thigh to knee and off, tears stinging my eyes, the pain immediate, extreme, and intense.

I looked at Anthony and tearfully said, "I can't do this. It hurts too damn bad."

He replied, "You're okay."

Was he nuts? I absolutely was *not* okay! I was in a nightmare. He gave me a moment and explained what was happening while I was getting it together.

Knots. I had knots. Lots of them. Apparently, when I had the stroke, all of the muscles of my body had not only seized up but also, they had completely twisted and knotted up. I instantly understood why I had felt like I was lying on hard plastic balls in the care facility. My body was loaded with knots in my muscles.

If this was any indication, odds were, this guy would kill me before the month was over. I went home that day, not all that happy, thinking the trial month I had given this *fine* endeavor could not end soon enough.

But later that day, the oddest thing happened; my legs didn't hurt quite as bad as the day before. That knot seemed to have eased up. I was amazed. Maybe this guy did know a thing or two.

Weeks turned to months, and I stuck to my new healthy eating lifestyle and workout plan. I could feel myself becoming stronger.

Soon, I no longer required a cane to walk, and, incredibly, the weight seemed to be falling off me.

Eventually, I bid my shower chair adieu and could now stand alone, safely in the shower. I was strong enough to get in and out of my incredible tub and would treat myself to a luxurious soak now and then. I had lost around 100 pounds, and life seemed to be getting better by the day.

On top of that, I started listening to myself more and making better decisions simply by listening to my gut. I was beginning to hear my intuition again. One evening, over dinner with friends at my house, a tidal wave of emotion came over me. It actually took my breath away, and I had to hold on.

Change! Undeniable change was coming; whatever it was, I knew it would be *big*. That was the first of many inklings I would get about the upcoming event that year. Monumental would be an understatement. I could feel it was coming. Approaching faster and faster. Whatever this was, the momentum of it was too huge to stop. It was inevitable and would change the lives of *many* people.

I could never quite figure out exactly what this colossal event might be, but each time, I accepted it a little more, knowing there was nothing I could do about it except roll with it. I understood that if I didn't, it would consume me.

How exactly do you prepare for the unknown? I could have never anticipated the chain of events that would come next.

Chapter Nineteen

Dad

My dad gifted me a golf cart so I could zip around the property and get my mail. He asked to see me one day in May 2016. I got in my cart, and off I went with a smile on my face.

As I entered his office, I could see his expression did not match mine. I thought maybe it was more shit with the county? He said he was going to have a meeting with all the staff the next day and wanted me there.

Okay, I thought.

"I'll be telling them that I have been diagnosed with inoperable lung cancer, and we'll need to sell the park."

I felt like I was hit with a cannonball. *Shell-shocked* is the best way to describe how I was feeling. "I wish—"

"I know," he said, but we can't go back. We can only go forward from here."

He was right. *Now* is exactly all we have.

I told my dad about alternative treatments and asked him to watch the documentary, *The Truth About Cancer*. Whatever course of action he decided on, I would support him. I'd want the same courtesy.

We had thirty-six people signed up to purchase their sites at Oak Tree Ranch and, according to our attorneys, we were able to start opening escrows in June—the very next month. The county had finally signed off on the application, and it was now in the hands of the state. Unfortunately, the attorneys neglected to tell us that the state had a *year* from June to complete their approval. It wouldn't be until the following June when we could close any escrow. Our funds being what they were, to wait that long was not feasible. Our long, costly efforts to sell the park to our residents ceased immediately.

My dad and I had discussed my ability to finish building out the ranch before we knew of his condition, but I just didn't have the stomach to deal with the county anymore. He went through painstaking measures to organize and set up a family partnership so this endeavor could continue, but it was all for naught. Still running a deficit since the fire in 2007, we had borrowed enough money to get us through June. There was no way, especially under these new circumstances, we could borrow any more.

The best offer was from a company that had repeatedly inquired about purchasing the property. After much consideration, my dad decided they would be the ones best suited to carry on. I did what I could to help prepare the mountains of documents that were required.

After weeks of nonstop gathering and copying of data, the task of closing all our businesses began. He handled the corporations and partnerships with the attorney, and I dealt with closing our dealership, canceling our licenses, and sending the documents to the appropriate agencies. It was all so surreal.

My dad was going to the doctor often; his wife, Deanne, was by his side each step of the way. Everybody wanted to spend time with him, but since I couldn't drive, I felt left out—almost pushed aside. I could never seem to pick a good time to see my dad in his home and coordinate it with someone who could take me. Someone was always there, or something was always going on. I didn't have the freedom or the means to make the time myself because I was always relying on someone else to drive me there.

Finally, Deanne and I worked out a weekly time, just for me, to see my dad. My friends really came through for me; it was a long haul up and back for an hour visit, which was about all he could tolerate in his condition. When he was hospitalized for the last time, my sweet cousin Barbara often drove well out of her way to bring me to visit him. Driving me there was a hardship for a number of loved ones like Barbara, but I am forever grateful to them. That time spent with him was priceless.

My dad had an opportunity that many do not. He was able to arrange his affairs exactly as he wanted. He had the opportunity to say goodbye and to spend time with the people he cared about.

As for me, I had the opportunity of a lifetime. After years of working so hard to get back to where I was, realizations filled me. A deluge of understanding flooded through me—first, a trickle, and then the floodgates opened—and the knowledge of all the lessons of my life filled my very being. Nothing was random. Every single thing I had been through made perfect sense. I could see it all for what it was.

My dad's dying process opened my eyes. He was *not* just my dad, a husband, a brother, an uncle, a grandpa. He was all those things—just like we all are. He was born, just as we all are, had hopes and dreams like we all do—fantastic victories, crushing defeats—and now, he would leave this Earth, just as we all eventually do.

I saw true love in action, and I was humbled.

Chapter Twenty

2020 And Beyond

Life has a momentum all its own that no force can ever stop. It might seem the death of someone you love would, at bare minimum, cause a slight pause of some kind in the continuum. That's just not the case. Life moves on. But then, there is no death. While the physical presence is no longer on this Earth, life goes on—forever.

After my dad died, I just kept moving forward, much like any of us do when facing life's ups and downs.

Like everyone, I had my share of struggles in 2018 and 2019. It was September of 2019 when my life started to crumble. The first obstacle was a small flood in my kitchen. A ten- gallon water heater under my bar failed, and voilà. This was the beginning of my home as a construction zone. Much like the days of negotiating the hospital visits with my dad, I did the best I could with my Bright Line Eating program.

My kitchen was a source of constant dust and debris, and the house was always cluttered. I simply could not keep up with the domino effect unfolding as the constant changes and endless work was done. It was impractical to eat at home anymore with the kitchen in the state it was. So, I ate out twice daily for nearly four months. I was a few pounds heavier when January 2020 rolled around.

Also at the turn of the year, my precious little boy cat, Big T, passed away. My sister, Debbie, came to stay with me in February, and it seemed as though the world had polarized on several levels shortly thereafter. My household, along with many others, was shaken up by what was transpiring in the world that year.

With vast changes in my personal life and the world at large, my thoughts easily shifted to focusing only on what was wrong.

Have you ever heard the phrase: *You get what you think about?* I was thinking doom and gloom, and guess what? I would go on to break the third and fourth toes on my right foot not once, not twice, but *three times*—before mid-year. I fractured the bone directly above my toes on the right foot—twice having my foot booted for a few months. In August, I dislocated my right patella for the first of many times that year. That was some serious pain.

As one might imagine, I was frustrated and not at all happy. My life was in a decidedly downward spiral. My body hurt, and the world was crazy. What else could happen? I *had* to ask.

I ended the year as a guest of Palomar Hospital for a few days—my heart having gone into A-fib—or beating irregularly—featuring blood pressure readings off the chart. What was going on? Maybe I just needed to stop and figure out my health. I had gone downhill fast.

As I looked back on the year, I realized I had also seen a great many people enter my life and just as many move out of my life for various reasons. *What* exactly *was going on?* That seems to have been the million-dollar question. I had gained a *lot* of weight over this year. I knew I was eating due to being extremely stressed out. But *why* was I stressed? I had virtually nothing to be stressed about.

It would take a few years, but eventually I figured it out: I am an empath. The stress I felt was not my own but from the world in chaos.

When I went to the other side following my stroke, I received the ultimate gift. My soul was made brand new. I got to see every single decision I had made that would form me into the human being that I became—that I am. Remembering this gift helped me understand. How could I have ever forgotten?

When we are children, our knowledge of the world is so very limited. We only know what our parents, siblings, and a small group of other family and friends tell and show us. As such, when the unexpected happens, it's not a stretch to think that our reactions would, in fact, be quite skewed.

Looking back, I decided at age three that I was bad. At age four, my body was something to be ashamed of. At age five, *nothing* I did was ever enough, and, by age six, whatever happened was my fault. It sounds ludicrous when said so simply, but those were the decisions I made. At those young ages, each of those events would have been too overwhelming for me to live with, so they were pushed into my subconscious mind. Running in the background and believing them true, my subconscious mind would do *anything* to keep me safe and my beliefs intact. All the decisions I've made have been based on four fundamental beliefs I had formed before the age of seven.

It's crazy how the subconscious mind works. Were these things true? Maybe yes, maybe no. It's how I saw it at the time; so, for me, they were. Mere moments in my childhood had become the foundation of my entire life. My subconscious mind unfortunately didn't get the 4-1-1. I don't know whether many people are blessed with understanding or even desire to look into the *why* of their thoughts and actions. I'm just lucky. I was gifted with not only understanding the *why* of my life, but also—and more importantly—the understanding that I can change it.

It's true that I had spent more than ten years since the stroke working hard to restore my abilities, but before the stroke, to put it bluntly, my life sucked. I lived, and apparently always had lived, in an atmosphere of extremely high stress. Yet, here I was, adding stressful situations to it daily. I did *not* want the life I had before. It was time for a new life, time to be my authentic self—unafraid and ready to share what I had without reservations.

I used to think I was no one special—except to people who loved me. I've come to understand that I *am* special. We are *all* special! We *all* came into this world with a gift to share. It's that thing we are—*or at least were*—passionate about. There are *no* exceptions. Everyone has something to offer. Some may have simply forgotten.

It's easy to get bogged down with life as I had, those *hidden beliefs* running the show. Life becomes too full of drama and somewhere along the line, we simply forget to take care of ourselves.

I was always too busy trying to fix everything and everybody else. I had spent my life believing my self-worth was defined by what I could do for others. In the early days at the care facility, my dad reminded me that all that mattered is that I am here. Had I already forgotten? I did have worth.

I forgot that I am a special being made to bring my gifts to this world. My gifts go by the wayside not wanting to stand out or shine. I know who I am now. I definitely took the scenic route to get here, but here I am. It's time for me to share my gifts, to share my truths.

I have searched my entire life for that illusive program, thing, secret knowledge, or whatever, that would bring me the love, peace, and comfort that I so craved. It has seemed like an eternity. *Surely, it's got to be big*, I thought. *Surely, it's hard to attain.* I finally figured it out. Here it is. The plain simple truth: it's love.

That's it.

Love is the answer to every single question or situation.

Everything any of us needs to know is within us. There is *nothing* outside yourself that will give you the answers you seek. The time is *now*. It's NOT what happened yesterday, last week, last month, last year, or decades ago; it is *now*. Nor is it what will happen tomorrow, the next day, the next year, etc. It's *now*. I'm not saying any of the programs or events I signed up for were useless. I love learning. But what I truly love is knowing the answers I seek are within me and that I have a direct communication with my all-loving Creator who made me. That is *love*.

My dad always appreciated this quote from an unknown source. We had it on the back of our business cards for years and I find it so perfect and so very true. It's just *now:*

Only One to a Customer

This bright new day

Complete with 24 hours,

Opportunities, choices and attitudes…

A perfectly matched set of 1440 minutes,

This unique gift, this one day,

Cannot be exchanged,

Replaced or refunded.

Handle it with care.

Make the most of it.

There is only one to a customer.

This is *it*. This one day truly *is* all we have. Take this day   you have and make the most of it. Spend some time looking within. It doesn't have to be hours of meditation, volumes of journaling, down on your knees in prayer for weeks. I'm not saying any of that is bad, but it certainly isn't necessary. Just start. Just begin.

You can start with five minutes. Go someplace where you can be alone that's quiet. Close your eyes and focus on your breathing. If your mind wanders, that's okay. Just bring your attention back to your breath. It gets easier the more you do this. You'll have that true communion with the one who made you. You'll be showered with love, and guidance will come in the way of thoughts and inspiration. You'll know without a shadow of a doubt, no matter what, everything will work out. There is no fear. How can there be?

I invite you to develop an awareness of exactly what you're thinking and saying. These things matter. Believe it or not, our words are powerful.

Are your thoughts and words kind and loving? Are they filled with joy?

Are you thinking about all the things that are *right* in your world?

Or are you thinking about what's wrong with your circumstances, your body, or the world? I always leaned toward the latter. So, it was no surprise that my life's path followed my negative thoughts. My mind was *filled* with constant chatter about circumstances out of my control, like how I'd respond to some imagined scenario. It's unreal what you might stumble upon when you start hearing all that goes on in your mind. Until you're aware, you can't stop it. It is vital that we each take that time for ourselves to get quiet and listen. It doesn't matter where you are, just start. It's *never* too late.

We live now, in this one day. Those things that have come before are gone. Each day we wake up, we have a choice of how our day will go. It's really that simple. We each choose what we will think and what we will say. Choose wisely. Remember, you can *always* change your mind and start over. There has *never* been a more crucial time for each of us to stand firmly in the love that we are, to shine our light from within, and to share the gifts we have been given. This one day can change everything.

Conclusion

My trip to the other side was so much more than a story to amaze. It was the opportunity of a lifetime. While there, I knew *everything*. I understood. Whereas the ways of the world are often out of our control, every soul has ties to something deeper. This we can know with as much certainty as we know the laws of gravity—that innate knowledge that we won't just fly away if we don't hold on to something.

During my dad's journey to his real home, I began to realize just how far I had come. I remember looking back on my life, starting when I was a young girl, and I realized I couldn't hear the way others did. My mostly silent world kept my innocence and purity intact for far longer than most ever enjoy.

I think back to when I was sixteen and had that conversation with my dad about quitting the fat camp. I could have given up because things got hard, or I could just keep going. Here I was, confronted with this same lesson again, on the road to recovery after the stroke. At any time, I could have determined it was too damned hard and given up. Had I given in to such a path, no doubt you would have found me in that wheelchair, parked in a corner to this day.

I began to realize that life is essentially good. It's all about how you manage your perspective. Though that might sound trite, it's absolutely the truth. You create your own reality by the thoughts you think and the words you tell yourself and others. Even when you are in the middle of incredibly difficult circumstances—a divorce, a bankruptcy, a stroke—you have the power to control the fear you feel and change the outcome.

I am no self-help guru, nor do I profess to have all the answers. I do not pretend to have some magical formula or easy fix to make life better or make your problems go away. My intent when writing this book was to share my life with as many people as I could. Based on the opportunities and experiences, I am blessed with a perspective worth offering. I have found hope, and I believe you can as well.

Eleven Lessons Learned

Lastly, I want to share some of the lessons I've learned along the way. By no means are they meant to predict what will work for you, but our divine Creator resides in each of us and guides us along our path, if we are willing to listen.

So, when you are challenged, when you are held in the grip of fear, when you don't know how you'll make it through another day, know this:

You can do it.

Allow me share some of the perspectives and lessons that have helped me:

Love

Above *all* else is love. Love is the answer to everything.

Awareness

Being aware is *huge*. I don't mean to suggest you should be looking over your shoulder; *self-awareness* means being aware of how you speak to yourself—the mind chatter.

Are you telling yourself how hard things are? Are you bemoaning your lack or time or money? Exactly how many times a day do you say the words: *I can't because I'm too busy* or *I don't have the time?* Is everyone else to blame for your circumstances?

Now is all we have. It does not matter how many times you verbalize, think about, or cry about something that happened yesterday; you must let go of what you cannot change. It's over. Change isn't always easy, but it certainly doesn't have to be hard. I wasted more than thirty years of my life blaming others before I finally became aware of what I was doing. No matter what your circumstances are, I just want to tell you to take a good look at— and listen to—what you're telling yourself each day. Your words have power, and they can change your world.

Gratitude

Gratitude is the most effective way to change your circumstances. Instead of focusing on or criticizing what's wrong, instead of trivializing your life, try starting your day with gratitude.

I start every day with words of gratitude. Before I even open my eyes, I put a smile on my face and just start speaking thanks for all the things that are right in my world—the sound my clock makes, the feel of soft, fresh sheets, my little furry cat, the fact I didn't have to lift a finger, and the sun came up—you get the idea.

Did my life's challenges go away because of that? No, they surely didn't. Yet, after starting my day with such sweet momentum, those things take a back seat and are not the center of my day as they once might have been. Quality of life increases in proportion to the gratitude in your heart.

Self-Love

There's a lot of talk these days about self-love. We know it's important, but how do we practice it in a way that doesn't seem trivial? How do we give it more meaning than a meme on social

175

media? How do we genuinely love ourselves—especially when we don't feel worthy of it because of the mistakes we've made?

With so many years of self-loathing under my belt, I know how challenging getting into the groove of self-love can be. It's kind of funny: I often hear people say: *Oh, I absolutely love myself.* Yet, their lives tell a different story.

Self-care—being gentle with yourself, shutting out the world, and taking care of your own needs first—is essential. I still struggle with this. My essential nature is to put others first. If we don't put ourselves first—if we don't take that time—at some point, we fail on many levels. Enter the stroke. Need I say more?

Not only did I fail to care for myself for so long, after the stroke I had no reserves left in me to care for anyone else, let alone myself. *Things like this don't happen to me*. That's what I used to think. Sound familiar?

Our Magnificent Bodies

One of the most sobering moments of my life was when I realized how poorly I had treated my body. Sadly, I know I'm not unique in this. It seems abusing our bodies is commonplace.

Where food is concerned, many of us feel forced to choose between convenience and nutrition. No one seems to have time to prepare a meal worthy of our bodies. The electronics revolution has left us sitting still and hardy ever moving our bodies. What's more, our minds are constantly stimulated instead of being used productively. Mindless screen time numbs us to just about everything and lulls us into a sedentary life that our magnificent bodies adjust to, because that's just what they do. Until, of course, they can't anymore.

I put too much stress on my body for too long. My poor food choices included high amounts of sugar and processed foods. And then there was the constant stress I was under because of all the scenarios playing out in my head all day. I was also taking between thirty to forty ibuprofens each day just to cope with my head and body aches. I smoked and carried around a massive amount of weight for years. I barely slept and drank copious amounts of coffee. Still, somehow my body kept moving. That is, until it had enough.

The massive stroke should have killed me. I was not expected to survive. I had, at best, a 13 percent chance of survival— and probably those were the odds ascribed to a much healthier person than I. And yet, for some reason my body just never gave up. I don't know that the medical professionals held any hope given my overall condition, but I am immensely grateful they used their time and talents to give me the best chance possible.

They say that after so many months, you've got about all you're going to get back functionally from such a health challenge. But here I am, still standing. While my recovery has not yet reached 100 percent, every day, every week, every month, and every year, I move forward. As I write this, I am still working to improve my visual and balance issues. I know that with time, they will be resolved completely. I no longer worry about it.

Right now, I'm learning to take things slowly and to watch as they unfold. I'm learning to react less and enjoy the process more. Sure, I fall back sometimes, but from where I was to where I am now, there is *no* comparison!

Meditation and Prayer

Prayer and meditation might be conceived as spending time with your Creator. It is a personal journey, unique to each individual. I will be bold here and assume that no matter what your religious or spiritual upbringing has been, we can agree there is a power much greater than ourselves.

I find it incredibly beneficial to spend time with my Creator. I like to do this in the morning, after I spend a bit of time luxuriating in gratitude. This is when I can move inside myself into the silent nothingness and not just listen, but actually *hear*. This is the place where inspired action is born. That divine being within is your gut that guides you every step of the way, if you choose to listen.

In my opinion, prayer is not just a set of memorized and rote words uttered without thought that many children are taught. For me, prayer is the giving of thanks—a celebration of those things and events we desire as if they are already here. I like to be grateful for all the blessings, whatever they might be, realized on this Earth or otherwise. I have found if I pray out of need or desperation, I actually get more need or desperation.

178

So, pray with a light heart and open mind, and you will be blessed with both.

Everything always works out for me.

So, when I ask for something or some situation in my prayers or meditation, and it seems like everything is going haywire and not at all like what I want, I try to remember a simple truth: things have a way of working out.

This may sound hard to believe, but I have found that you must let go of the fear of certain outcomes. You must have faith and trust that perhaps your Creator might know a thing or two you do not. He might not need your help in producing a desired outcome. Most people are control freaks. Having spent many a year trying to control everything, I know it's not an easy one to give up. But it works, and it's worth it.

The Answers Are Within

Before the stroke of luck that took me to the other side and back, I always looked outside myself for answers. I always felt like the answers to the challenges I was facing or the dreams I wanted to create were always someplace else.

My journey to the other side made me realize that my inner guidance system had been working loud and clear all along. I had turned a deaf ear to it and ignored my intuition. I didn't trust that everything would work out. I had prayed for a husband and in walked Steve. I told myself it *had* to be him. My gut said no, but I couldn't see anything else, and so I didn't listen. I turned off that voice that kept telling me it was a big mistake.

Well, that was a big mistake. I got to see that on the other side. I got to see how life would have been if I had only followed my own guidance system, which has my best interest at heart. I got to see every single time I ignored my intuition and what life would have been like, had I followed it. It was one of the most sobering experiences ever. The takeaway: trust your gut. Read that again:

Trust your gut.

That Something We All Carry

When I was in the arms of my Heavenly Father going through the review of my soul, I was shown that we are all the same. We all have that *something*—those things in our lives we are proud of, ashamed of, or hurt by.

When my dad was dying, I could see this in his own life. I could see he was once a baby. He was once a young boy. He had felt heartbreak. He had felt defeat. He had had the ups and the downs that we all have. His was just a different series of events.

We are all the same. It doesn't matter who you are or what you do, we all have challenges we will face, obstacles we will overcome. Once you understand that we are all the same, it's incredibly liberating. There's no jealousy, there's no envy, there's no need to wish you were somewhere else where the grass looks greener. We are all in the green grass right now. It's all in how you look at it.

If you're showing gratitude for where you are, for the people in your life—regardless of whether they're treating you right or wrong—then you are in control. The negative people in your life can be your best teachers. They can show you the kind of people you *do* want in your life. Your focus creates your reality. You can see yourself as separate, alone, and victimized, or you can see the blessings in disguise.

Don't Expect People to Get You

For much of my life, I wanted people to *get* me. I wanted them to understand who I am and where I'm coming from. I wanted everybody to be happy, to the point that I thought it was my job to make everyone happy. I wanted them to love me for me. But I've realized to do that means my happiness depends on what someone else thinks. It simply doesn't work like that. Your happiness is your own responsibility.

Not everyone is going to like you or get you. Half the time, we don't even understand ourselves. So, how can we expect that of another person?

In the end, the only thing that matters is that you get yourself and that you know that your Creator gets you—because He does.

Don't be bothered by the people who don't get you. They're too busy thinking about themselves anyway.

Life

This life is a gift. Going to the other side and back made me realize that in ways I don't know how to perfectly articulate. Life here is meant to be experienced. We have the opportunity here to create everything that we experience. When you understand that, you realize you have the power to turn almost anything around—no matter how shitty the circumstance is. Our thoughts create our reality.

And in this earthly opportunity, we can create anything we want. Good, bad, crazy, beautiful. We can smell, feel, touch, taste, and hear things on this side that aren't the same on the other side.

I believe we have chosen to come to these earthly bodies in order to experience certain things, almost like we purchased a ticket to come on the journey here, so that we can experience different parts of ourselves and evolve.

The "F Word"

After the divorce, I carried around a tremendous hatred toward Steve. I refused to Forgive him. Ah, the difficult "F Word." I held on to that hatred for decades. I felt like it was my mission to get my vengeance on him. I wanted him to suffer. I thought he deserved it.

I remember one day, decades after the divorce but before the stroke, I came home from work and sat down to pray. It was the first time in a very long time that I had sat down in the silence. And that's when I heard a very clear voice say to me, "Are you done yet?"

I felt something change in me. I thought: *Yes, I'm done*. It felt like the weight of a piano had been lifted off me.

That was the first layer of my healing. The first step is to begin to forgive the people that have hurt us. That doesn't mean that you excuse what they've done or justify it, but that you choose to let them go.

The second, and most important, layer of that healing came during my journey to the other side. I saw how I had essentially shredded my soul with all the hatred that I had toward Steve over those years. This is why the second layer is so important: to forgive yourself. That is the ultimate act of forgiveness.

We like to project our hurts, pains, and traumas on other people. They have their part in it, of course, but forgiving ourselves for allowing ourselves to be traumatized by that experience—by not honoring ourselves afterward, by not listening to our gut, or whatever it may be—is the radical act. That is the true art of forgiveness. It's your reaction to what they do that is what's important. If somebody hates you, hurts you, or mistreats you, how do you choose to react? Realize the choice is in your hands. When you choose, now you have the power.

You can change the environment. You can rewrite what the story means. You can choose to let life still be good. Ultimately, it's not what happens to us that matters, it's that we choose to forgive ourselves again and again and choose to take the lessons from the experience. Believe me, you are worth it.

Next Steps

So, what's next for you?

You may want to partake in a rather lengthy scenic route, much as I did. On reflection, I can't honestly say I'd recommend it. I have no course you could study nor any miraculous how-to method to propel you where you are going based on what I've tried. I find it's not exactly a one-size-fits-all kind of world.

The absolute truth is, we all have everything we need inside us. Life is an even playing field. Not one person possesses more or less than another of what is required to live a happy, fulfilled life, able to pursue any dream they wish to follow. The only criteria, as far as I can see, is you have to want it.

You *can* do anything you want to. The answer will always be love.

About the Author

Brenda Caster has studied energy healing for decades, long before a stroke entered her experience. She became certified and practiced energy healing at a spiritualist church in the San Diego area. She also studied under Dr. Bradley Nelson, becoming certified as an Emotion Code Practitioner and Body Code Practitioner. She continues to strengthen her talents to better assist others, helping them let go of what holds them back so they might live their best, authentic life.

Brenda is a member of several communities that offer deep connection, transformation, and encouragement in realms of spiritual and creative endeavors, including an intention group, a dream-weaving group, and a quilting group. She has been living in the Ramona, California area for approximately twenty years, enjoying the country atmosphere and hometown feel of this friendly little town. Her creativity expands to painting murals in her home and crafting in just about any medium. Brenda enjoys her garden, spending as much time as possible in it. She also enjoys design and helped plan her indoor and outdoor living spaces, including a Fairyland fire pit area and the *angelic realm*, a space to sit and reflect and enjoy the surrounding beauty.

Brenda has designed and is fine-tuning her next project called *Hidden Acres*. Her plan is to develop an active senior community that has expanded to a small, self-contained city.

To say it is an ambitious plan might be an understatement. When completed, she believes it will become a model for similar communities and could be implemented anywhere in the United States—possibly the world.